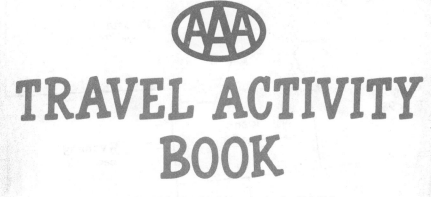

TRAVEL ACTIVITY BOOK

THE OFFICIAL AAA FUN BOOK FOR KIDS

by Tom Koken, Jane Lipp,
and Kathleen Paton

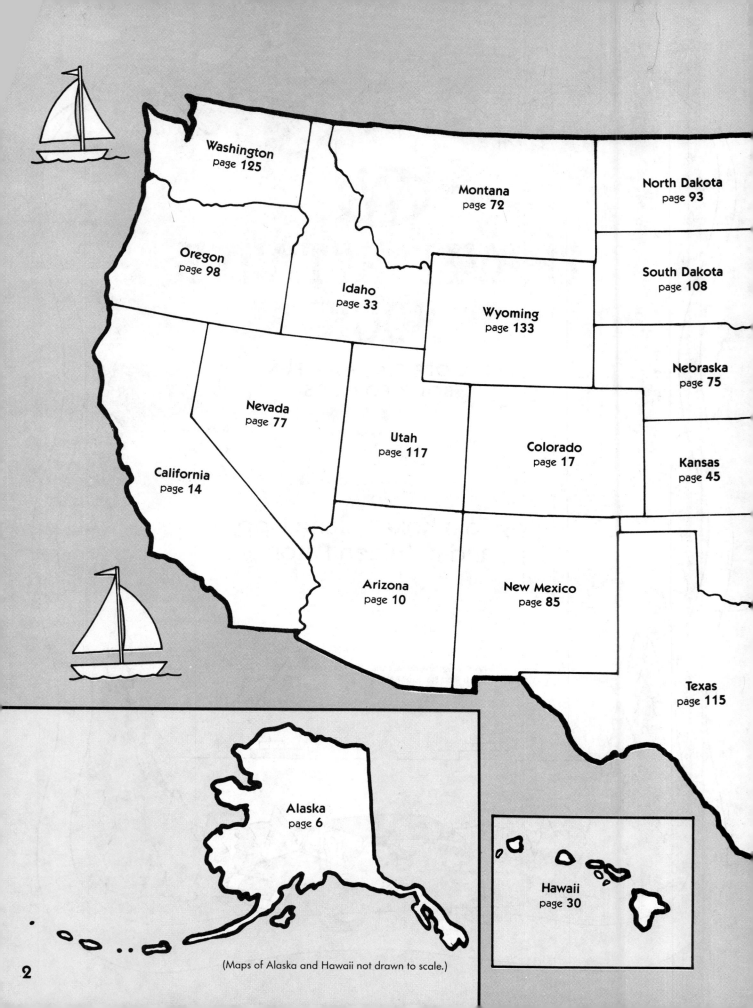

Washington
page **125**

Montana
page **72**

North Dakota
page **93**

Oregon
page **98**

Idaho
page **33**

Wyoming
page **133**

South Dakota
page **108**

Nevada
page **77**

Utah
page **117**

Colorado
page **17**

Nebraska
page **75**

California
page **14**

Kansas
page **45**

Arizona
page **10**

New Mexico
page **85**

Texas
page **115**

Alaska
page **6**

Hawaii
page **30**

(Maps of Alaska and Hawaii not drawn to scale.)

Minnesota page 65
Wisconsin page 130
Michigan page 63
New Hampshire page 78
Maine page 55
Vermont page 121
New York page 86
Massachusetts page 59
Rhode Island page 105
Connecticut page 20
Pennsylvania page 103
New Jersey page 82
Delaware page 22
Maryland page 56
Iowa page 43
Ohio page 94
West Virginia page 128
Virginia page 123
Illinois page 37
Indiana page 38
Missouri page 70
Kentucky page 48
North Carolina page 89
Tennessee page 110
South Carolina page 106
Oklahoma page 97
Arkansas page 13
Georgia page 29
Mississippi page 67
Alabama page 5
Louisiana page 50
Florida page 26

In this book, you will find games and activities for each of the fifty states. The page numbers on the map above show which page each state is on. Color the state after you have done the activity. (Answers to all the puzzles begin on page 137.)

TRAVEL

How many words can you make from the letters in "TRAVEL"?
Use each letter only once in each word.

_____ _____

_____ _____

_____ _____

_____ _____

_____ _____

_____ _____

_____ _____

_____ _____

_____ _____

_____ _____

ALABAMA

Here is a map of Alabama and some of its cities and towns. You may have heard of Montgomery, the capital, or Birmingham, but have you heard of Bird Eye? Bird Eye is located at B-6 on the map. To find B-6, go across the top or bottom of the map and find B. Then go down one side of the map and find 6. Where these two lines meet is B-6.

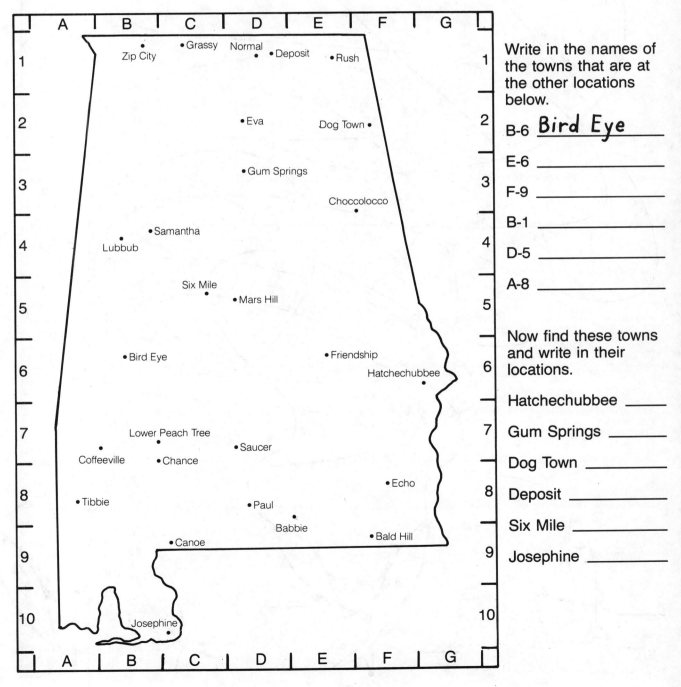

Write in the names of the towns that are at the other locations below.

B-6 _Bird Eye_

E-6 _____

F-9 _____

B-1 _____

D-5 _____

A-8 _____

Now find these towns and write in their locations.

Hatchechubbee _____

Gum Springs _____

Dog Town _____

Deposit _____

Six Mile _____

Josephine _____

Alaska has one of the biggest fishing industries in the United States. The fishing lines below are all tangled. Match each to its pole and write the number of the pole next to each fish.

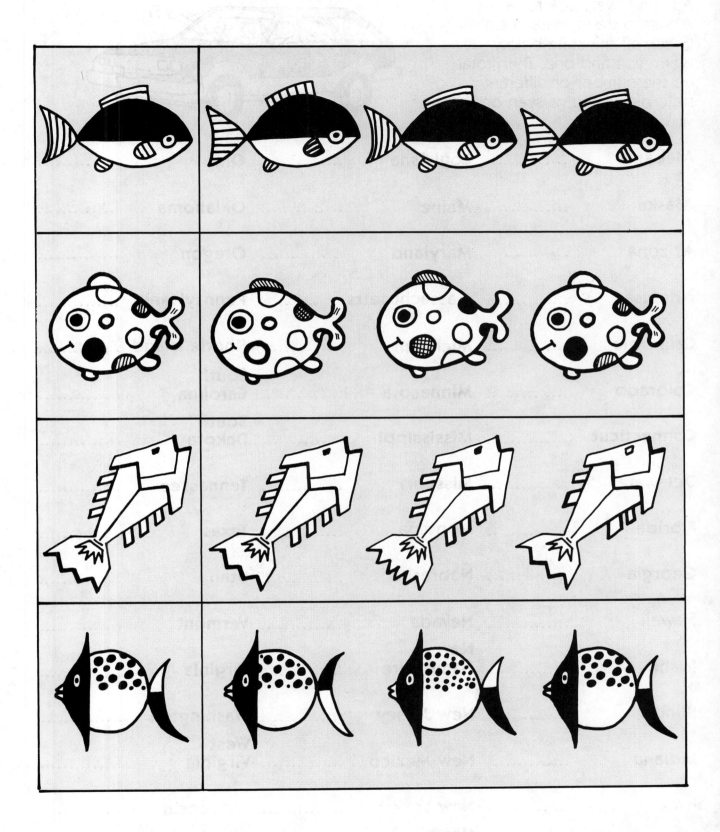

In each row draw a circle around the fish that is exactly the same as the fish in the box to its left.

As you travel, look for a license plate from each state. Check off the state below when you find one. Then total up the number of different state plates you've seen on your trip.

Alabama	....	**Louisiana**	....	**Ohio**	....
Alaska	....	**Maine**	....	**Oklahoma**	....
Arizona	....	**Maryland**	....	**Oregon**	....
Arkansas		**Massachusetts**	....	**Pennsylvania**	....
California	....	**Michigan**	....	**Rhode Island**	....
Colorado	....	**Minnesota**	....	**South Carolina**	....
Connecticut	....	**Mississippi**	....	**South Dakota**	....
Delaware	....	**Missouri**	....	**Tennessee**	....
Florida	....	**Montana**	....	**Texas**	....
Georgia	....	**Nebraska**	....	**Utah**	....
Hawaii	....	**Nevada**	....	**Vermont**	....
Idaho	....	**New Hampshire**	....	**Virginia**	....
Illinois	....	**New Jersey**	....	**Washington**	....
Indiana	....	**New Mexico**	....	**West Virginia**	....
Iowa	....	**New York**	....	**Wisconsin**	....
Kansas	....	**North Carolina**	....	**Wyoming**	....
Kentucky		**North Dakota**		**TOTAL**	....

Ralph can't find some of the things he had packed for his vacation. Help him find his book, comb, sock, sunglasses, and toothbrush.

ARIZONA

Arizona has many kinds of cacti. The largest is the giant Saguaro cactus, which can grow up to fifty feet high. Its white blossom is Arizona's state flower. Connect the dots and then color the picture.

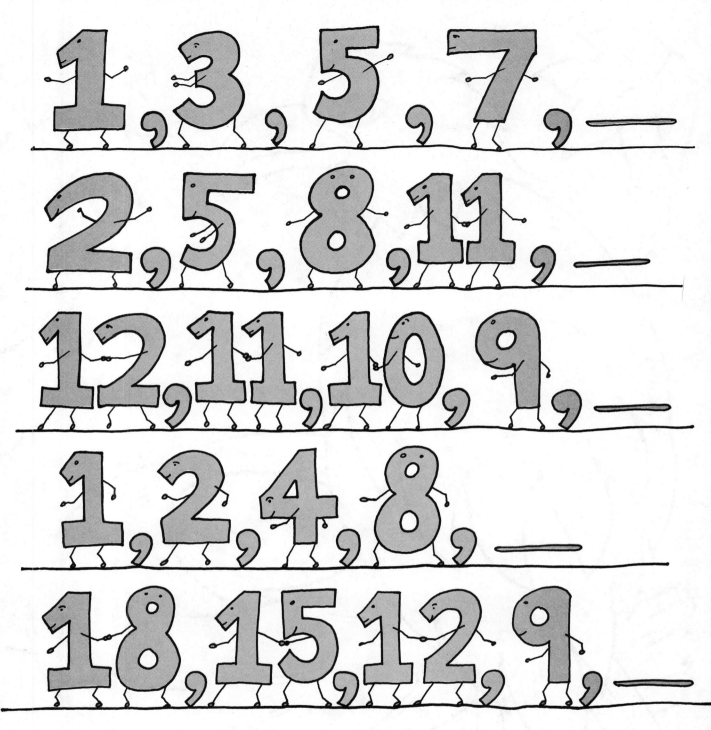

1, 3, 5, 7, ___

2, 5, 8, 11, ___

12, 11, 10, 9, ___

1, 2, 4, 8, ___

18, 15, 12, 9, ___

Look at each row of numbers above. From the numbers below, choose which number comes next in each row. Write it in the blank.

8   16   6   14   9

The bald eagle is a symbol of the United States. Here is one for you to color.

L+ -B   + ANSAS   -E+ CAUSE

We _____ _____ _____ of:

....

LITTLE

_____ _____

....

MY+ -K   -T+ VERN

_____   _____

....

-YON +TER

_____ of _____

....

_____   _____

This rebus gives four special reasons to visit a southern state. To find the answers, spell out each picture and add or subtract the letters shown. Write the words in the blanks below each picture.

On this map of California the names of some cities have been scrambled. Unscramble each name and write it on the line provided. The list of cities in the box will help you.

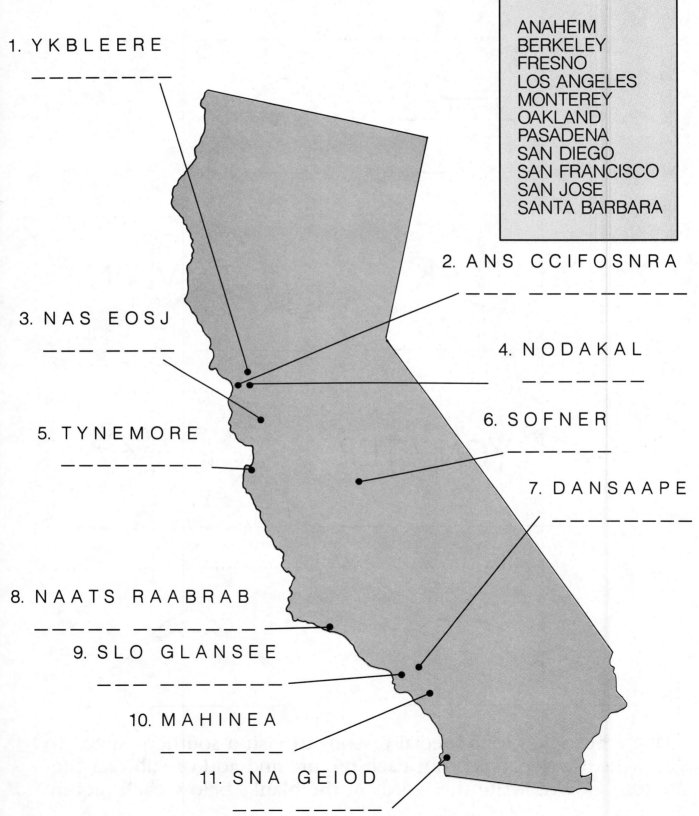

ANAHEIM
BERKELEY
FRESNO
LOS ANGELES
MONTEREY
OAKLAND
PASADENA
SAN DIEGO
SAN FRANCISCO
SAN JOSE
SANTA BARBARA

1. Y K B L E E R E

_ _ _ _ _ _ _ _

2. A N S   C C I F O S N R A

_ _ _   _ _ _ _ _ _ _ _ _

3. N A S   E O S J

_ _ _   _ _ _ _

4. N O D A K A L

_ _ _ _ _ _ _

5. T Y N E M O R E

_ _ _ _ _ _ _ _

6. S O F N E R

_ _ _ _ _ _

7. D A N S A A P E

_ _ _ _ _ _ _ _

8. N A A T S   R A A B R A B

_ _ _ _ _   _ _ _ _ _ _ _

9. S L O   G L A N S E E

_ _ _   _ _ _ _ _ _ _

10. M A H I N E A

_ _ _ _ _ _ _

11. S N A   G E I O D

_ _ _   _ _ _ _ _

These building blocks are A-OK! See if you can fill each set of blocks horizontally with a word that fits. For example, the top two blocks can be filled with the word "at."

Find your lucky number!

1	2	3	4	5	6	7	8	9
I	H	G	F	E	D	C	B	A
R	Q	P	O	N	M	L	K	J
	Z	Y	X	W	V	U	T	S

HERE'S HOW: Let's say your name is Tom Brown. Using the chart above, write down the number for each letter in your name.

T	O	M		B	R	O	W	N
8	4	6		8	1	4	5	5

Then add it all up.

8+4+6=18   8+1+4+5+5=23

Keep adding 18 to 23 to equal 41.

Then add 4 to 1 to equal 5.

Tom Brown's lucky number is 5.

Now try it with your own name.

COLORADO

Colorado is a great place for skiing. There are some strange things happening on these slopes. Can you find all eleven of them?

Bill needs a key to start his car. Help him through the maze to get the key.

The cars above were rented from Mona Helen's Rent-a-Car on Friday. Five cars were returned on Monday. Circle the car above that is still out.

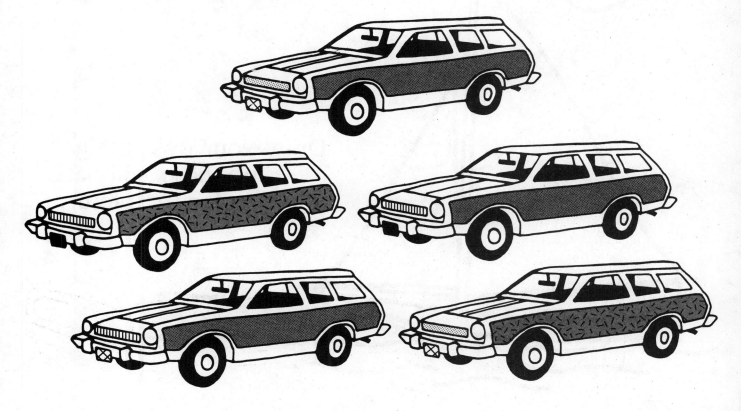

CONNECTICUT

Ship building and sea trade were very important in the growth of Connecticut. One shipyard was at Mystic. Beautiful, fast sailing ships called clipper ships were built there. Today Mystic is a popular spot for pleasure boats.

Draw your own designs on these sailboats. Then color the picture.

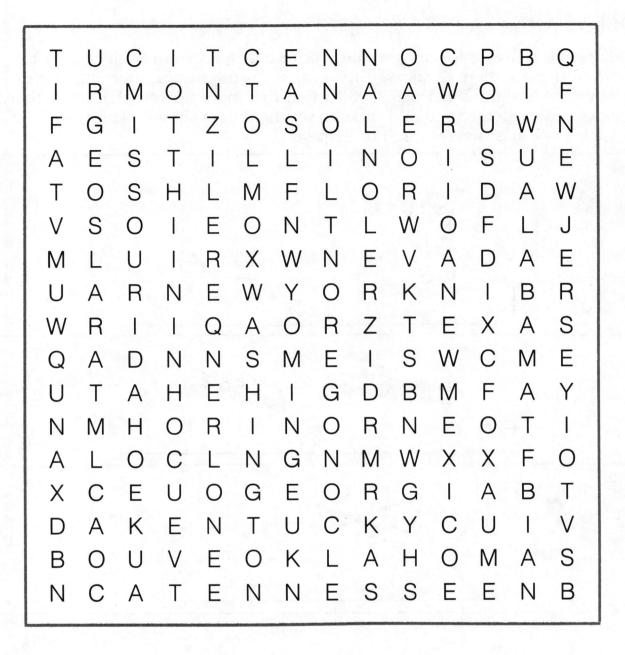

```
T U C I T C E N N O C P B Q
I R M O N T A N A A A W O I F
F G I T Z O S O L E R U W N
A E S T I L L I N O I S U E
T O S H L M F L O R I D A W
V S O I E O N T L W O F L J
M L U I R X W N E V A D A E
U A R N E W Y O R K N I B R
W R I I Q A O R Z T E X A S
Q A D N N S M E I S W C M E
U T A H E H I G D B M F A Y
N M H O R I N O R N E O T I
A L O C L N G N M W X X F O
X C E U O G E O R G I A B T
D A K E N T U C K Y C U I V
B O U V E O K L A H O M A S
N C A T E N N E S S E E N B
```

There are 24 states in the puzzle above. They are written up, down, forward, backward, and diagonally. How many can you find?

ALABAMA	IOWA	NEVADA	OREGON
CALIFORNIA	ILLINOIS	NEW JERSEY	TENNESSEE
CONNECTICUT	KENTUCKY	NEW MEXICO	TEXAS
FLORIDA	MAINE	NEW YORK	UTAH
GEORGIA	MISSOURI	OHIO	WASHINGTON
IDAHO	MONTANA	OKLAHOMA	WYOMING

DELAWARE

Delaware is a flower-lover's paradise because flowers from both the North and South grow there. Azaleas, Turk's caps, buttonbushes, morning glories, and water lilies grow in Delaware. To find five more flowers that grow there, spell out each picture and add or subtract the letters shown. The first letter of each word has been written to help you.

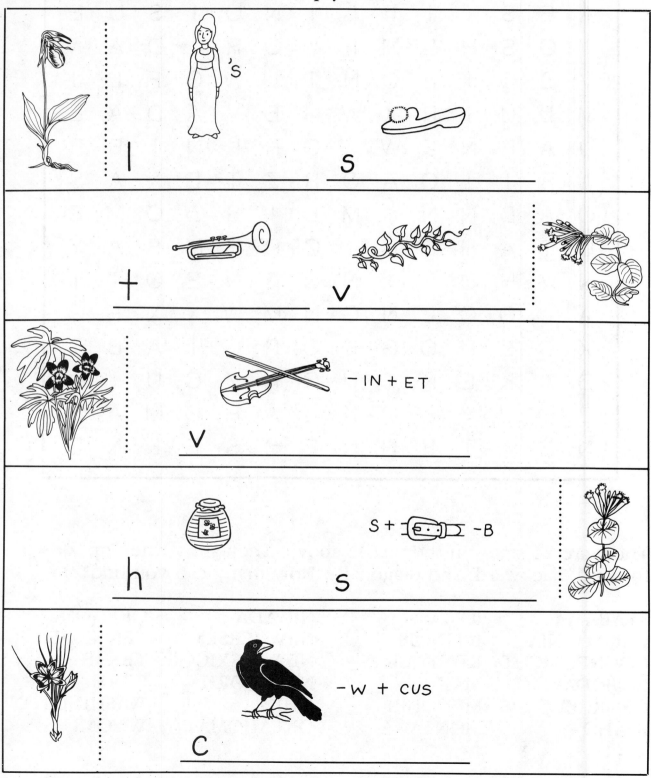

Color the picture.

NOODLE Doodles

Instructions

This is a game for two or more players. The first person asks for an adjective, noun, verb or whatever the space calls for. The other player(s) then call out words which the first player writes in the blank spaces in the story. When all the spaces are filled in, the story is read aloud. The results can be very funny.

The Noodle family is planning a vacation. There's Mr. and Mrs. Noodle, Judy, Rudy, and

Stroodle, the Noodle poodle.

"Where would you like to go?" Mr. Noodle asks his family.

"I want to go see the _____ _____ of _____. I
               ADJECTIVE   PLURAL NOUN   CITY OR TOWN

hear they're very _____," says Judy.
          ADJECTIVE

"Let's go to _____," says Mrs. Noodle. "I want to shop for
        CITY OR TOWN

_____ and take pictures of the _____ _____."
  PLURAL NOUN   ADJECTIVE   PLURAL NOUN

"How about you, Rudy?" asks Mr. Noodle.

"I want to go _____ in the _____ waters of Lake
     VERB ENDING IN "ING"   ADJECTIVE

_____," says Rudy.
  NOUN

"Well, the sooner we get going the more we'll see," says Mrs. Noodle. "Let's start packing.

Judy, Rudy, remember to bring your _____ and plenty of _____.
                       NOUN   PLURAL NOUN

I'll pack some _____ to eat in the car."
      PLURAL NOUN

"Let's go!" say the Noodles.

An adjective describes something or somebody—small, greedy, beautiful.

An adverb tells how something is done and often ends in "ly"—quickly, happily, carefully.

A noun is the name of a person, place, or thing—car, elbow, boy.

A verb is an action word—jump, fly, throw.

As the Noodles drive along they pass the time in different ways. They sing

"_____ Bottles of _____ on the Wall." They count how many
    NUMBER   LIQUID

_____ they see outside. When Judy gets tired she _____ in the
   PLURAL NOUN   VERB ENDING IN "S"

back seat, while Rudy _____ out the window. The Noodle poodle chews on
                          VERB ENDING IN "S"

his _____, and Mr. and Mrs. Noodle listen to a _____
       NOUN   ADJECTIVE

_____ on the radio.
   NOUN

At lunchtime the Noodles go to the International House of _____. Mr.
                                                       PLURAL NOUN

Noodle is very _____, so he orders the "_____ Man Special."
              ADJECTIVE   ADJECTIVE

Mrs. Noodle gets a hamburger with extra _____ on the side. Rudy and Judy
                                        PLURAL NOUN

split a peanut butter and _____ sandwich.
                     NOUN

The Noodles spend the rest of the day camping out. First, they set up their

_____ tent. Next, the children go _____ while Mr. Noodle
   ADJECTIVE   VERB ENDING IN "ING"

collects kindling and Mrs. Noodle prepares the _____ for dinner.
                                        NOUN

After Mr. Noodle gets a _____ fire going, he puts a pot of
                         ADJECTIVE

_____ on to boil, then throws in the _____ to cook. While the
   LIQUID   NOUN

meal is cooking, the Noodle poodle catches the scent of a _____ and goes
                                                      NOUN

running after it. Finally the Noodles sit down to eat. Rudy exclaims, "This dinner is

_____!"
   ADJECTIVE

"Yes," agrees Mrs. Noodle. "Everything tastes _____ when you are eating
                                              ADJECTIVE

outdoors."

Florida

Below are pictures of things that have to do with Florida. Look at the page for a few minutes. Now close the book and see how many things you can remember.

Pink
Flamingo

Sunglasses

Palm
Tree

Alligator

Citrus
Fruits

Beach
Umbrella

Convertible

Play this memory teaser by yourself or with other players. Using the categories along the top, fill in the boxes below with words starting with the letters in the left-hand column. The first line has been done to help you get started.

	Fruit or Vegetable	Television Show	Boy's or Girl's Name
P	Peach	Pee Wee's Playhouse	Patty
L			
A			
Y			
G			
A			
M			
E			
S			

Between the 1820s and 1850s a style of architecture called Greek Revival became very popular in the United States. One reason is that democracy was very important in ancient Greece and Americans wanted their buildings to be symbols of democracy. They even gave some towns Greek names—such as Athens, Georgia, and Ithaca, New York. Many Greek Revival buildings look like temples and have big columns and triangle shapes over doors and windows. Often the buildings are painted white. As you travel, look for Greek Revival buildings that are banks, museums, city halls, or houses. Keep track of how many you see in each category on the score card below.

Banks	Museums	City Halls	Houses

  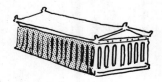

GEORGIA

CLAY
COTTON
GRANITE
PEACHES
PEANUTS
PECANS
SHRIMP
SOYBEANS
TOBACCO

P	O	M	R
E	A	F	D
T	C	X	N
B	H	E	S

Y	O	B	U
T	R	A	Z
C	F	C	P
M	O	C	W

D	F	E	C
Y	B	G	A
O	V	N	T
S	B	S	Q

W	P	O	C
A	T	S	X
T	U	B	R
M	O	N	V

N	I	M	P
C	R	W	L
Y	H	O	R
S	Q	A	B

C	P	H	L
F	E	R	X
A	K	G	J
N	U	T	S

K	A	W	J
N	P	R	G
I	T	O	F
B	E	C	U

S	N	Z	G
C	V	A	F
J	T	C	B
M	R	E	P

H	M	C	S
N	L	Q	G
I	A	T	D
Y	B	X	R

Georgia has a mild, sunny climate and produces many things.
With your pencil or crayon, draw a line from one box to another,
spelling out the Georgia products listed in the peanut above.
Follow the arrows.

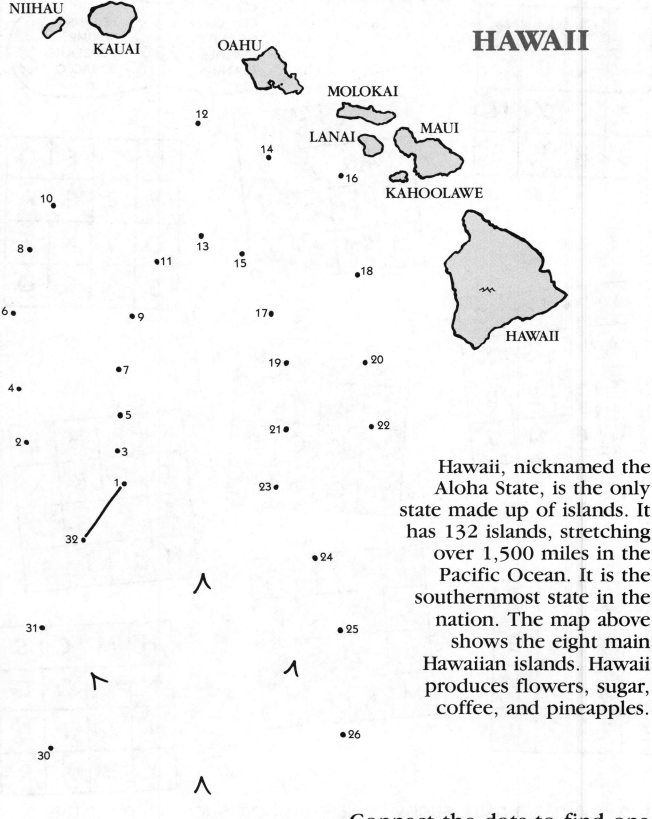

HAWAII

NIIHAU

KAUAI

OAHU

MOLOKAI

LANAI   MAUI

KAHOOLAWE

HAWAII

Hawaii, nicknamed the Aloha State, is the only state made up of islands. It has 132 islands, stretching over 1,500 miles in the Pacific Ocean. It is the southernmost state in the nation. The map above shows the eight main Hawaiian islands. Hawaii produces flowers, sugar, coffee, and pineapples.

Connect the dots to find one of Hawaii's most famous products.

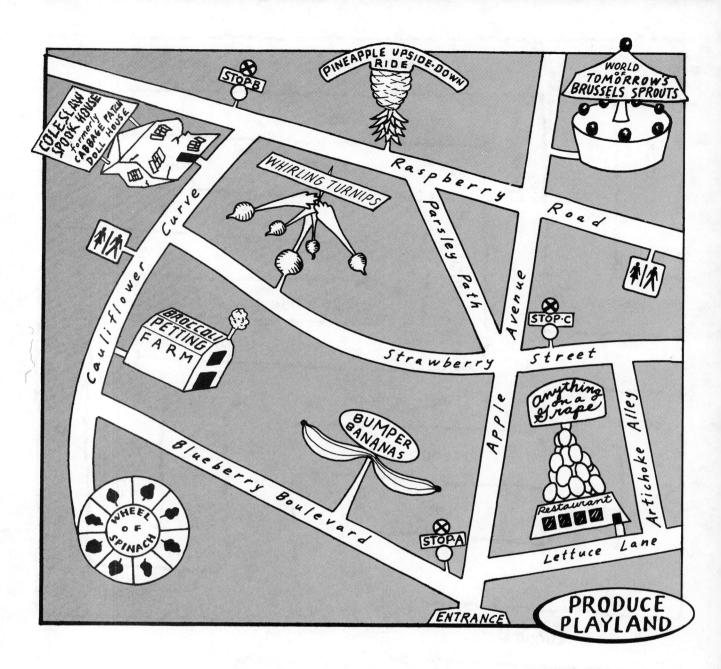

The Onionbergs went to their favorite theme park, Produce Playland. With your crayon or pencil, draw on the map above to help them find their way around.

1. What's the fastest route to Pineapple Upside-Down Ride from the entrance?
2. After the ride the Onionbergs wanted to visit a restroom. Which one is the closest?
3. A scary walk through the Coleslaw Spook House made the Onionbergs hungry. They decided to take the trolley to Anything on a Grape. If they board the trolley at Stop B, will they be closer to the restaurant entrance by getting off at Stop A or Stop C?
4. After lunch they decided to split up. Billy went to the Whirling Turnips. Mr. Onionberg went to try his luck at the Wheel of Spinach. Mrs. Onionberg went to hear the Brussels Sprouts sing. If they all walk at the same speed who will get to his destination first?

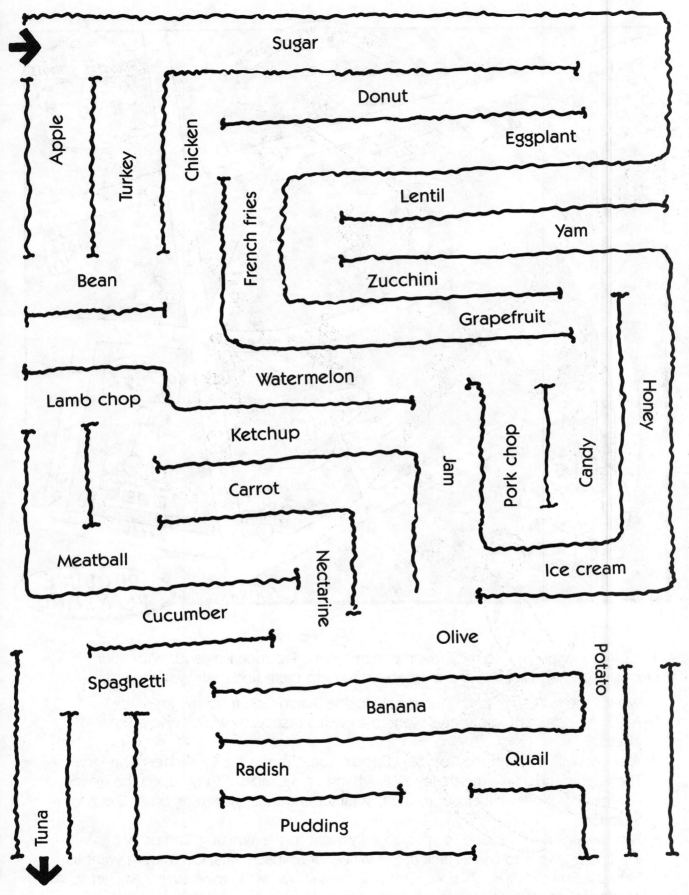

Eat your way alphabetically through this maze!
(CLUE: Start with "apple" and end with "tuna.")

IDAHO

Idaho grows billions of potatoes every year, more than any other state. Look at this scene at La Potato Palace. There are some strange things happening here. Circle all eight of them.

AMERICAN BIRDS

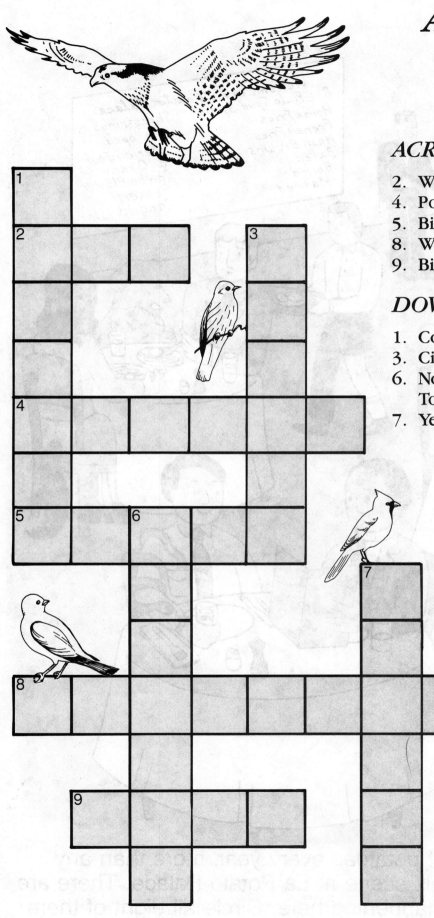

ACROSS

2. Wise bird
4. Popular bird at Thanksgiving
5. Bird with a red breast
8. Wild game bird
9. Bird of prey

DOWN

1. Country alarm clock bird
3. City-living bird
6. North American bird or Toronto baseball player
7. Yellow songbird

Color the picture.

These two apple trees look alike, but there are seven things that make the bottom tree different from the top tree. Find them and circle them.

Illinois is known as the Land of Lincoln because Abraham Lincoln lived there most of his life. He was born in Kentucky in 1809. Although he had very little schooling, he became a lawyer. In 1861 Abraham Lincoln became our sixteenth president.

ACROSS

2. A person who is "owned"
4. Mary _____, Lincoln's wife to be
8. Union soldiers fought _____ soldiers
10. Lincoln's age two years before he became president
11. Illinois: _____ of Lincoln
12. Lincoln's profession before he was in politics
15. _____ cabin
16. Mr. and Mrs. Lincoln went to Ford's Theater to watch a _____.
17. Capital of the United States of America

DOWN

1. The "Bluegrass State"
2. Capital of Illinois
3. John _____ Booth
5. Completed or ended
6. Small house in the country
7. _____, writing, and arithmetic
9. To free the slaves
13. Thanksgiving dish: candied _____
14. Red-breasted bird

INDIANA

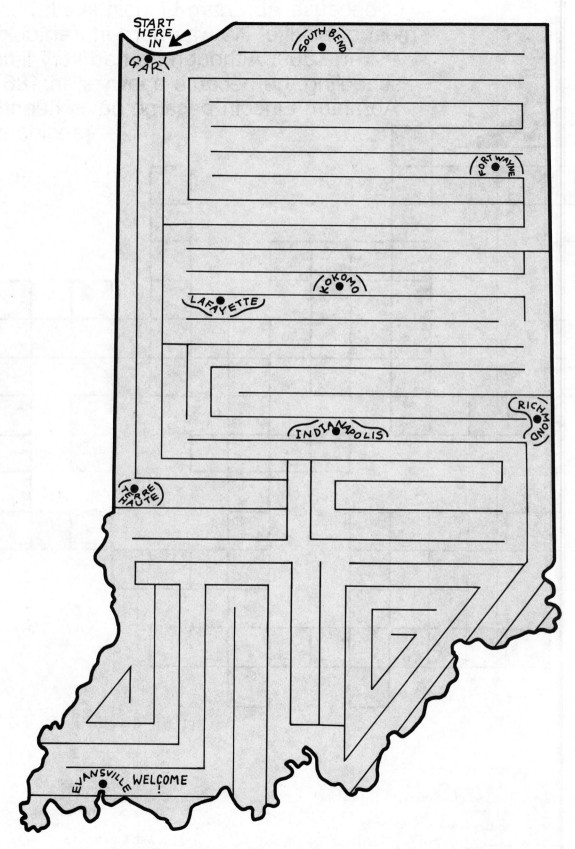

In Indiana, the "Hoosier State," it's easy to go from Gary to Evansville, but not so easy when you can't go through any other town. Try it!

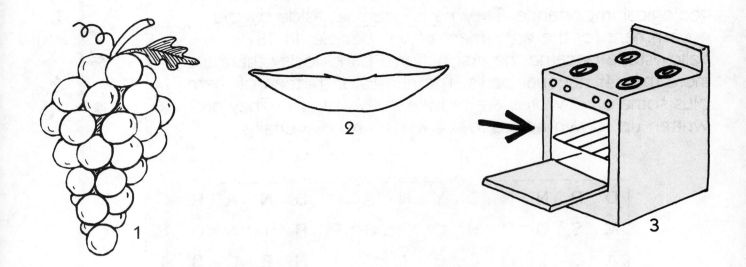

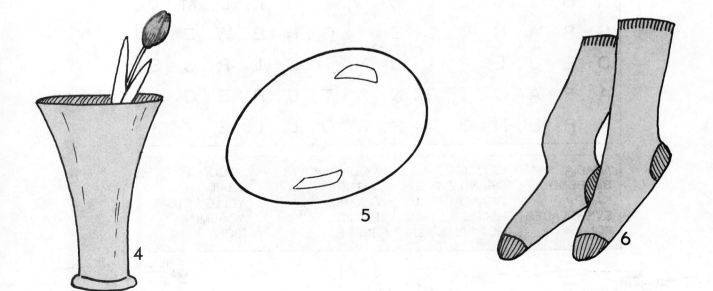

In the cold of winter what do you need on hand? In the spaces above, write the first letter of each word that describes each picture.

Our national parks are areas of great beauty and historic and geological importance. They have been set aside by the government for the enjoyment of the people. In 1872, Yellowstone became the first national park. Today there are more than 45 national parks. The names of thirteen of them plus some other words are hidden in this puzzle. They are written up, down, across, backwards, and diagonally.

YOSEMITE

```
D  R  N  N  O  Y  N  A  C  D  N  A  R  G
M  S  O  P  H  O  T  S  P  R  I  N  G  S
A  O  L  Q  E  B  I  C  I  N  E  C  S  I
S  L  U  D  F  V  Z  R  P  O  Z  C  L  O
T  Y  A  N  D  S  E  Q  U  O  I  A  R  R
H  M  P  E  T  A  B  R  L  S  O  M  A  E
I  P  L  B  I  M  U  T  G  W  N  P  E  I
K  I  C  G  E  A  C  O  R  L  E  S  T  C
I  C  L  I  A  R  T  K  A  C  A  D  I  A
N  O  S  B  L  U  W  C  I  U  K  D  M  L
G  R  A  N  D  T  E  T  O  N  B  W  E  G
D  E  U  L  P  I  C  N  I  C  L  R  S  S
A  F  A  O  T  G  N  A  T  U  R  E  O  L
K  R  E  N  O  T  S  W  O  L  L  E  Y  P
```

ACADIA	GLACIER	MOUNT MCKINLEY	SEQUOIA
BIG BEND	GRAND CANYON	NATURE	TRAIL
CAMP	GRAND TETON	OLYMPIC	YELLOWSTONE
EVERGLADES	HIKING	PICNIC	YOSEMITE
FUN	HOT SPRINGS	SCENIC	ZION

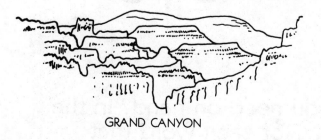

GRAND CANYON

SEQUOIA

GOING CAMPING

There are many hiking trails and campgrounds in our national parks. Rangers help to take care of the parks. They teach visitors about the local plants and animals, and how to protect the balance of nature in the parks. Visitors must not feed wild animals or pick flowers or remove anything from the parks, not even a little rock. They must be careful with cigarettes and matches. Fires should be built in fire pits and never left unattended. Visitors must always leave their campsites clean.

What is the Dumm family doing wrong? Look at the picture below and see how many things you can find.

The Map Code

Hidden in this map of the United States is a secret message. The first letter of each numbered state is a letter of the secret message. For example, the state marked 1 is Washington. Put a W in the first space below. When you have done this with all eleven states, you will know the message.

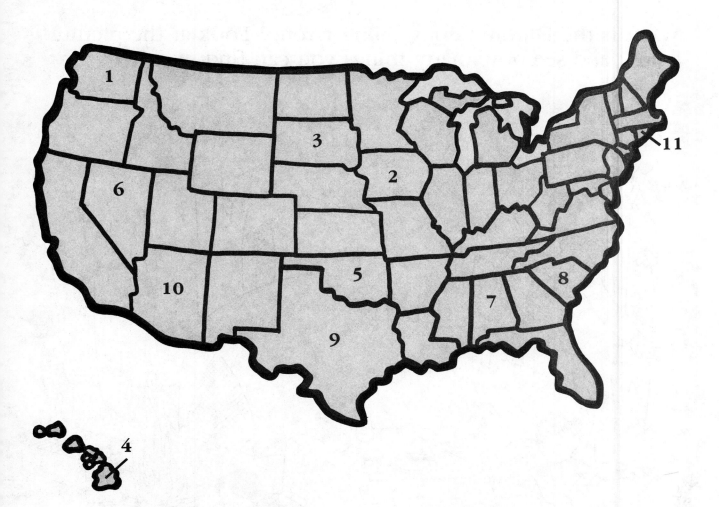

‾‾‾ ‾‾‾ ‾‾‾ ‾‾‾   ‾‾‾ ‾‾‾   ‾‾‾   ‾‾‾ ‾‾‾ ‾‾‾ ‾‾‾
 1   2   3   4   5   6   7   8   9   10   11

Corn is one of the most valuable crops grown in the United States. Iowa grows more corn than any other state. About $^3/_5$ of the corn goes to feed animals. Many nonedible products are also made from corn.

These two puzzles are filled with corn products. The top ear has things we eat, and the bottom ear has things we don't eat. Find the words in the lists below. The words go up, down, across, backwards, and diagonally.

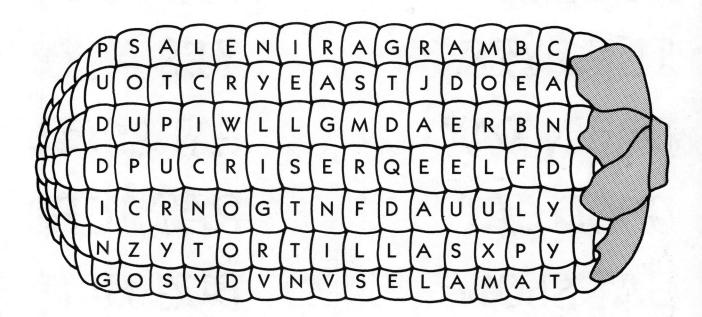

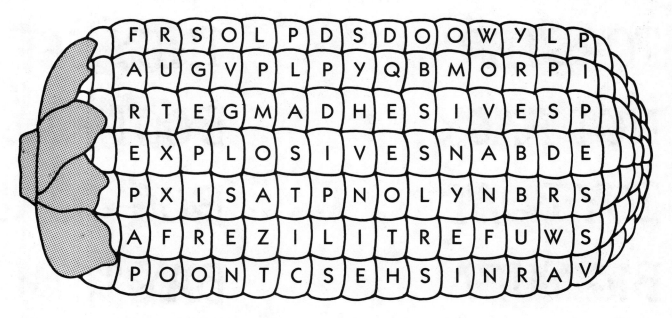

THINGS WE EAT		
BREAD	MARGARINE	SYRUP
CANDY	OIL	TAMALES
CEREALS	POPCORN	TORTILLAS
GRITS	PUDDING	VINEGAR
JELLY	SOUP	YEAST

THINGS WE DON'T EAT		
ADHESIVES	FUEL	PLASTIC
DYES	NYLON	PLYWOOD
EXPLOSIVES	PAINTS	RUBBER
FERTILIZER	PAPER	SOAPS
FILM	PIPES	VARNISHES

FAST CAR	TOE SLAW
ROOT BAG	DAD YAWN
THE EYES	YES A TON
DAWN DAY	FAT SCAR
GOOD CAT	RAT TOES
EAT SLOW	BUG BAIT
TOASTER	THEY SEE
NOT EASY	BOOT RAG
TOY BOAT	DOG COAT
BIG TUBA	BAY TOOT

An anagram is a word or phrase made by rearranging the letters of another word or phrase. Draw a line from each phrase on the left to its anagram on the right.

KANSAS

Color all the triangles in this picture. When you are finished, you will see a scene from Kansas.

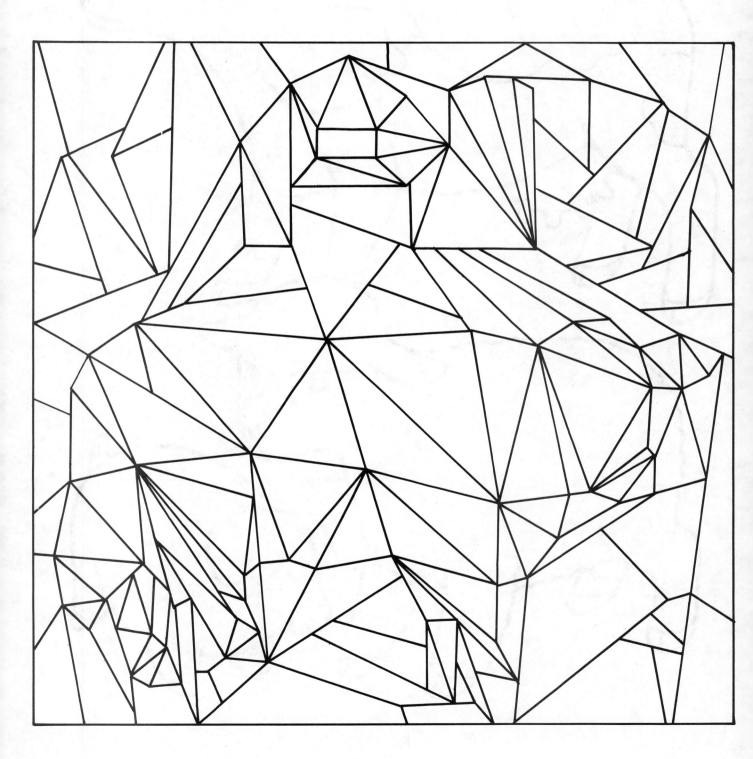

Color the picture.

Color the picture.

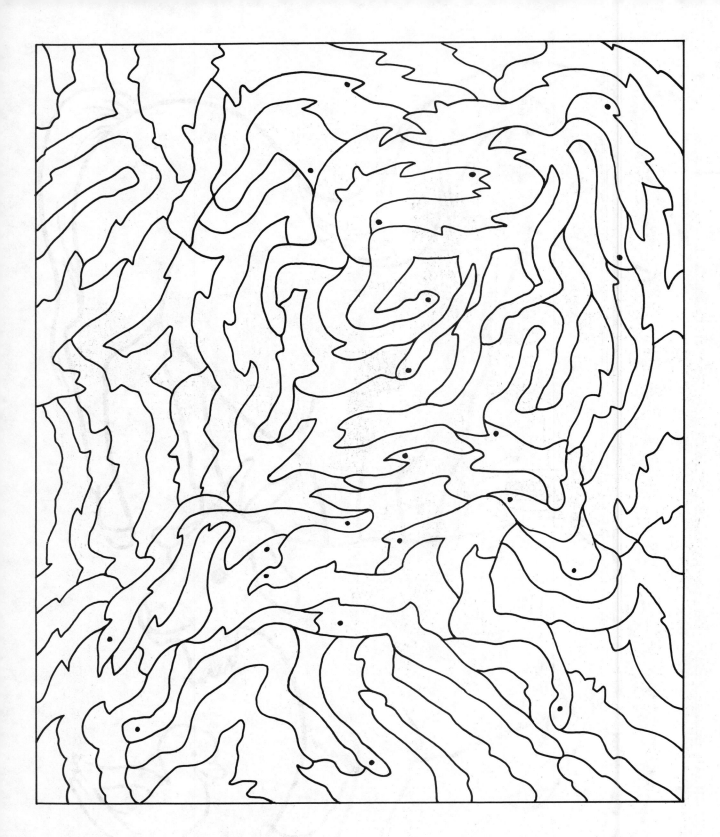

KENTUCKY

Kentucky is famous for its bluegrass and is known as the Bluegrass State. But it is also famous for something else. Color all the shapes in the picture without dots and you will discover what it is.

While the Bibbles were out sightseeing, a maid came to tidy up their hotel room. The top picture shows what their room looked like when they left. The bottom picture shows what it looked like when they came back. Circle the 17 things that prove the maid was there.

LOUISIANA

The largest city in Louisiana is New Orleans. Every year millions of people come to New Orleans to celebrate Mardi Gras, which takes place in February or March. There is always a big parade with floats and people dressed up in fancy costumes and disguises. These people are going to Mardi Gras. Draw a line from each person above to their costumed self below.

Here are four faces for you to dress up and disguise for Mardi Gras.

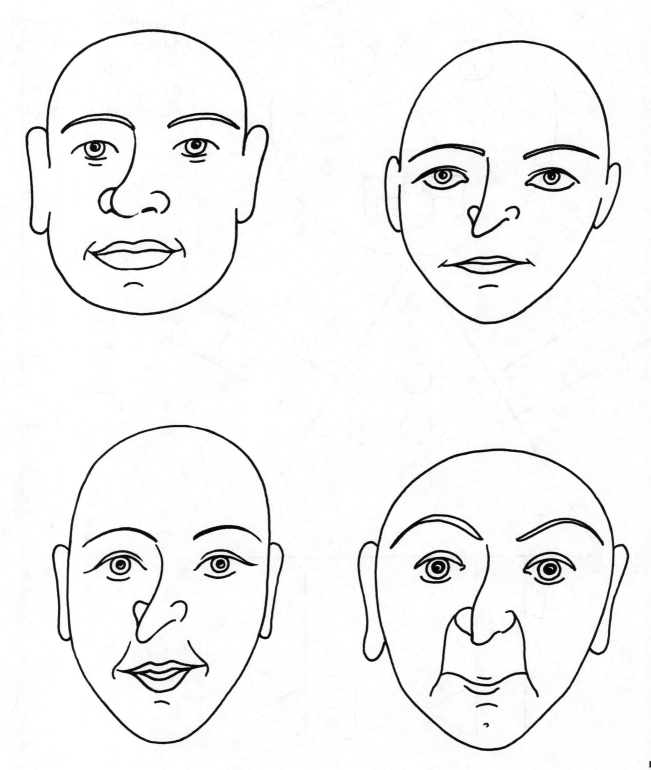

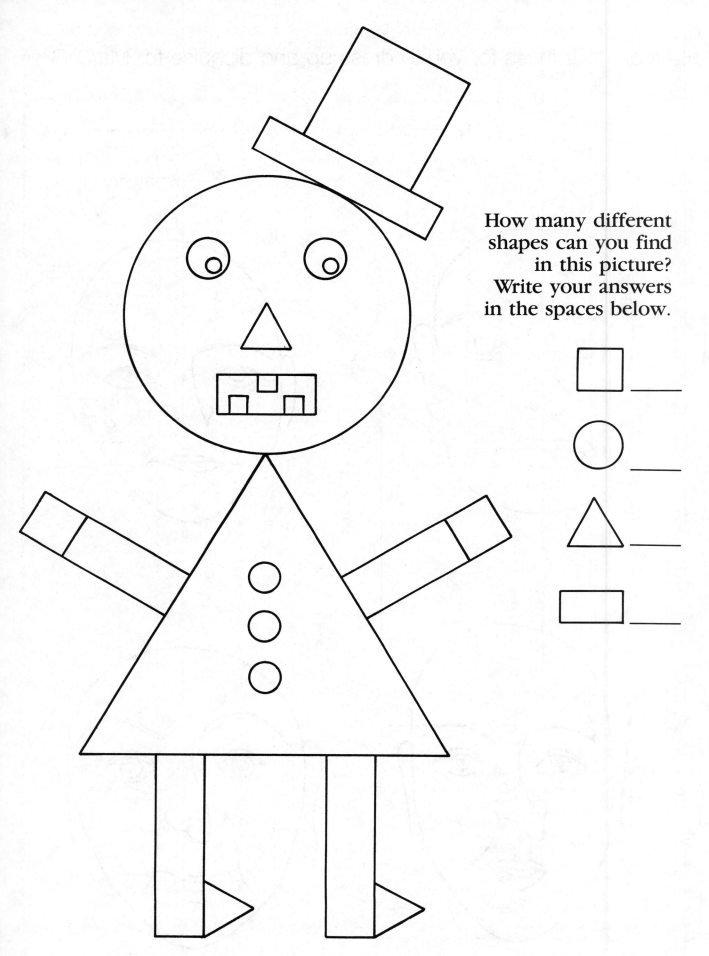

How many different shapes can you find in this picture? Write your answers in the spaces below.

The travel-weary Shmern family is looking for a nice place to spend the night. Use your pencil or crayon to find the most direct route to the Palace Resort.

Color the picture.

Maine has some of the best fishing in the Atlantic Ocean, so many of its early settlers were fishermen. Today fishing is still an important industry there. Connect the dots to see what most Maine fishermen hope to catch. Then color the picture.

Maryland, our seventh state, is almost cut in two by the Chesapeake Bay. This state is famous for Maryland blue claw crabs. Look at the crabs below and draw a circle around the two that are exactly alike.

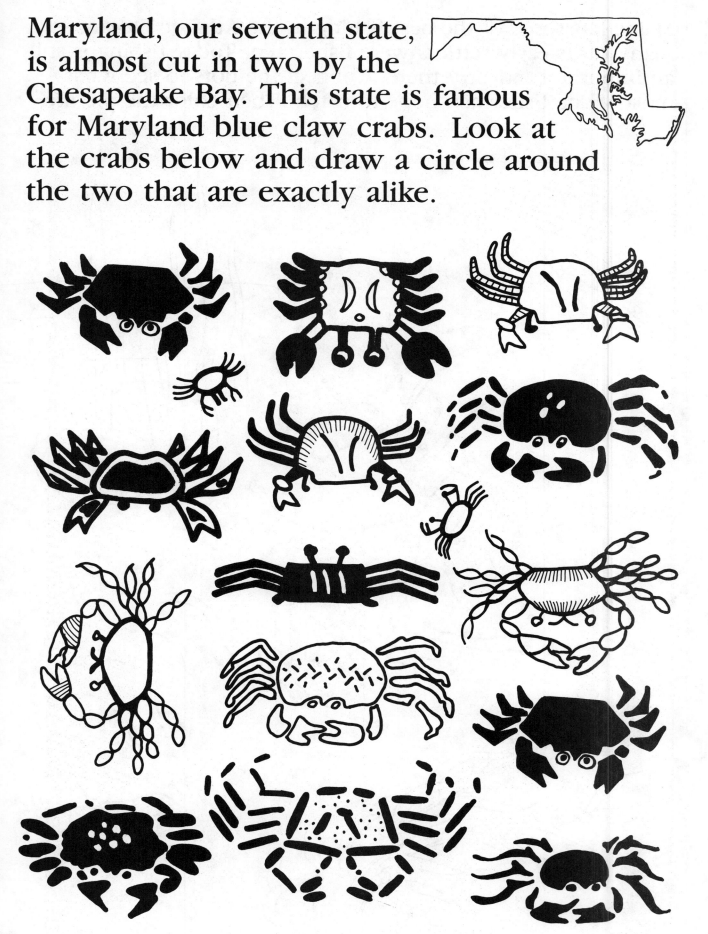

Color the picture.

BE A WORD MAGICIAN

Change LOVE to MILK. Do this by changing one letter in the word LOVE to make a new word. Write the new word in the blank spaces next to LOVE. Continue making new words by changing only one letter at a time until you spell MILK. Now try changing BOTH to EARS.

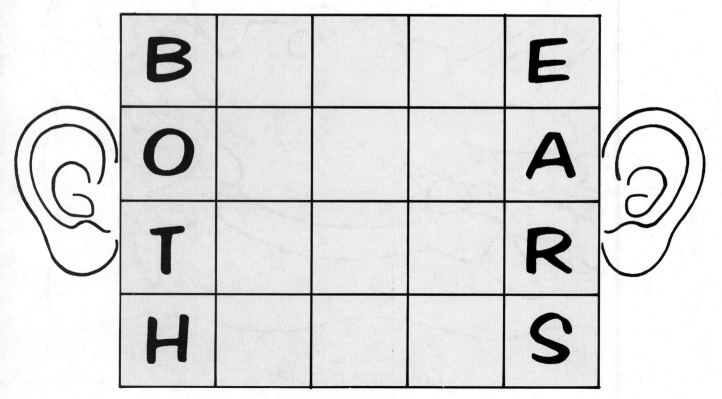

CONCORD

LEXINGTON

MASSACHUSETTS

In 1775, Paul Revere made his famous ride from Boston, Massachusetts, to Lexington and Concord. He brought a warning to Samuel Adams and John Hancock that British troops were coming.
Help Paul Revere get to Lexington and then Concord.

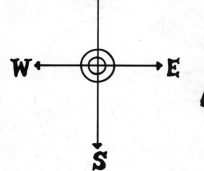

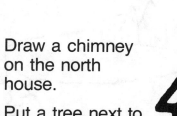

Draw a chimney on the north house.

Put a tree next to the south house.

Color the door of the east house

Draw a path up to the west house.

The House
That Jack Built

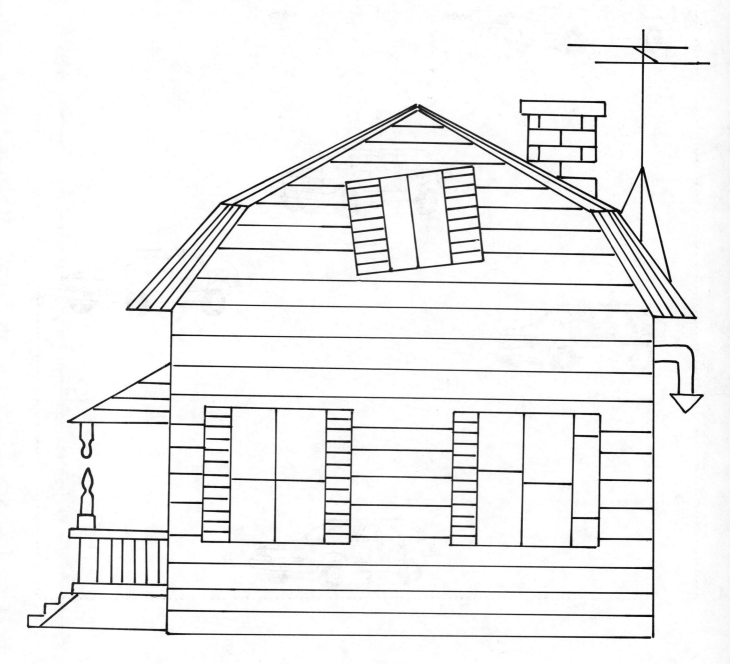

Jack Careless built this house. He made a lot of mistakes.
Can you find all six of them?

By drawing only three straight lines across the square, separate each car from the others.

1912
Detroit

1986
Ford Escort

1958
Plymouth

1947
Lincoln Continental
Cabriolet

1928
Model A Ford

Detroit is the largest city in Michigan. Over sixty percent of America's cars are made there. Here are cars from five different periods. Draw a line from each car to its name and the year it was made.

Where Does It Come From?

Each famous object pictured below can be found in an American city. Can you name them and the cities where they can be seen?

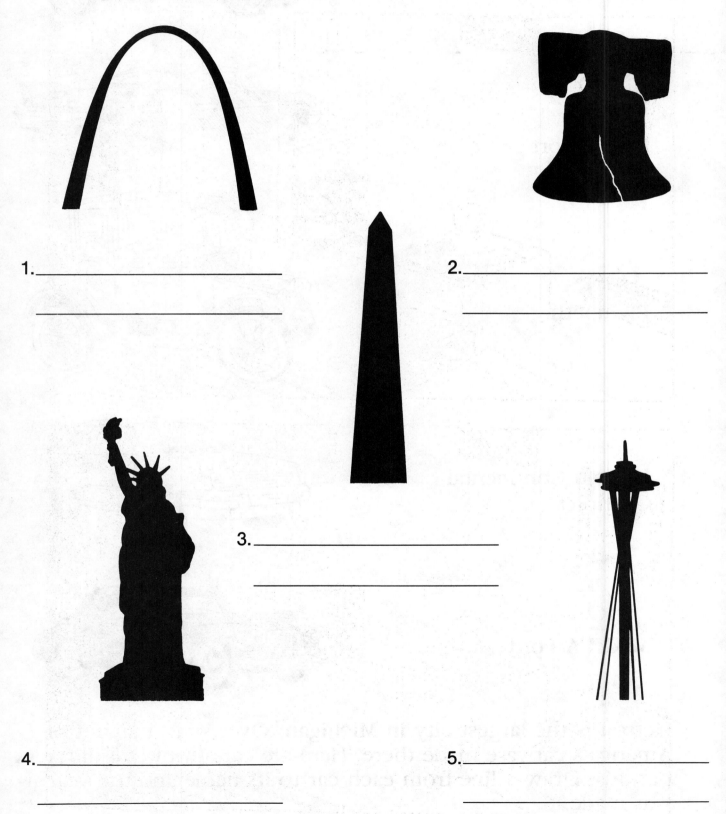

1._____

_____

2._____

_____

3._____

_____

4._____

_____

5._____

_____

MINNESOTA

Minnesota is nicknamed the Land of 10,000 Lakes, but it actually has more than 15,000 lakes and many rivers. Minneapolis is its largest city. Help this canoeist find his way from the twin cities of Minneapolis and St. Paul back to his cabin in the woods. He can travel from lake to lake through connecting rivers, but he can only travel across lakes where the numbers equal seven.

This squirrel has stored some acorns for the winter. Now he wants to find them. Use your pencil or crayon to help him.

MISSISSIPPI

The state of Mississippi is named after the great river that makes up its western border. The Mississippi River is the longest river in the United States — 2,348 miles. It has always been important for transportation in the areas through which it flows.

Find the eight rivers in Mississippi state and the other words listed below in the puzzle. Read up, down, forward, backwards, and diagonally.

```
H O B T N E R R U C T R A B E
S S P A D D L E M H O S W I M
I P P I S S I S S I M O H G D
F M Q U P R E L T C W C V B N
S U N F L O W E R K T A S L E
O D R E V I R L P A E G R A B
U D C A N O E R H S B O U C O
R E F L O O D A W A T E R K A
C L P O N C L E D W Z P N L T
E T Z E T L A P R H I A O U M
P A S C A G O U L A B R G H P
Y A L T D L E A F Y N I S A B
```

BARGE	CHICKASAWHAY	MISSISSIPPI	SUNFLOWER
BANK	CURRENT	MUD	SWIM
BASIN	DELTA	PADDLE	TALLAHATCHIE
BEND	FISH	PASCAGOULA	TUG
BIG BLACK	FLOOD	PEARL	WATER
BOAT	FLOW	RIVER	YAZOO
CANOE	LEAF	SOURCE	

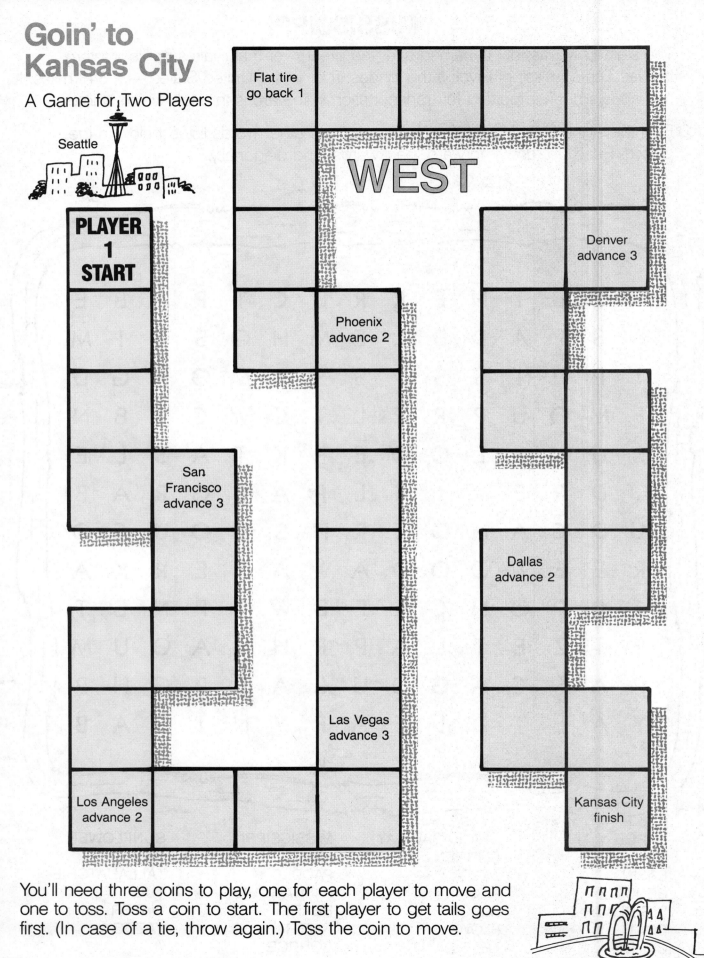

Goin' to Kansas City

A Game for Two Players

Seattle

PLAYER 1 START

WEST

Flat tire go back 1

Denver advance 3

Phoenix advance 2

San Francisco advance 3

Dallas advance 2

Las Vegas advance 3

Los Angeles advance 2

Kansas City finish

You'll need three coins to play, one for each player to move and one to toss. Toss a coin to start. The first player to get tails goes first. (In case of a tie, throw again.) Toss the coin to move.

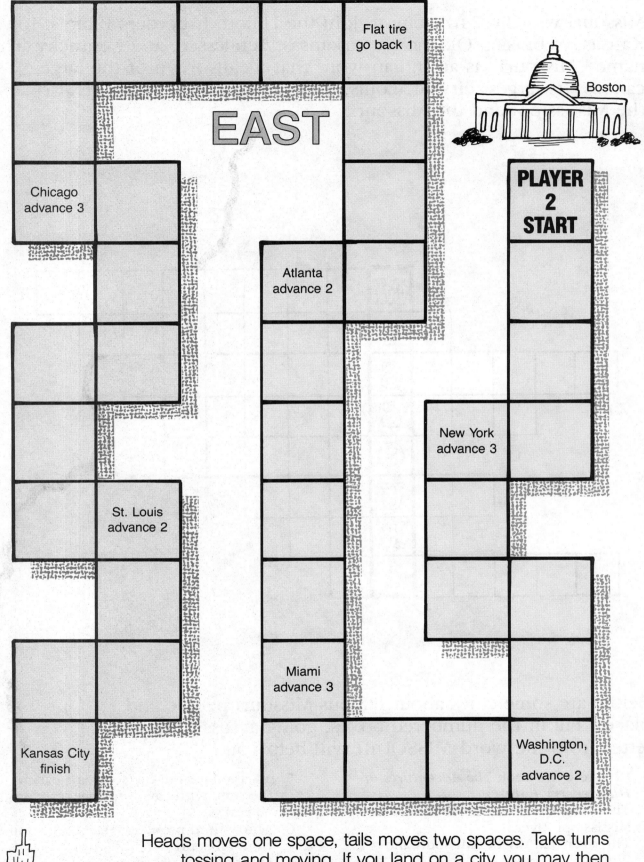

Flat tire
go back 1

EAST

Boston

PLAYER
2
START

Chicago
advance 3

Atlanta
advance 2

New York
advance 3

St. Louis
advance 2

Miami
advance 3

Kansas City
finish

Washington,
D.C.
advance 2

Heads moves one space, tails moves two spaces. Take turns
tossing and moving. If you land on a city, you may then
advance the number in that space. The first player to reach
Kansas City wins.

MISSOURI

Missouri was the 24th state to join the Union. It borders Illinois, Iowa, Kansas, Nebraska, Oklahoma, Arkansas, Tennessee, and Kentucky. The name "Missouri" is an Indian word that means town of the large canoes. Its largest city, St. Louis, is at the junction of two great rivers, the Mississippi and the Missouri.

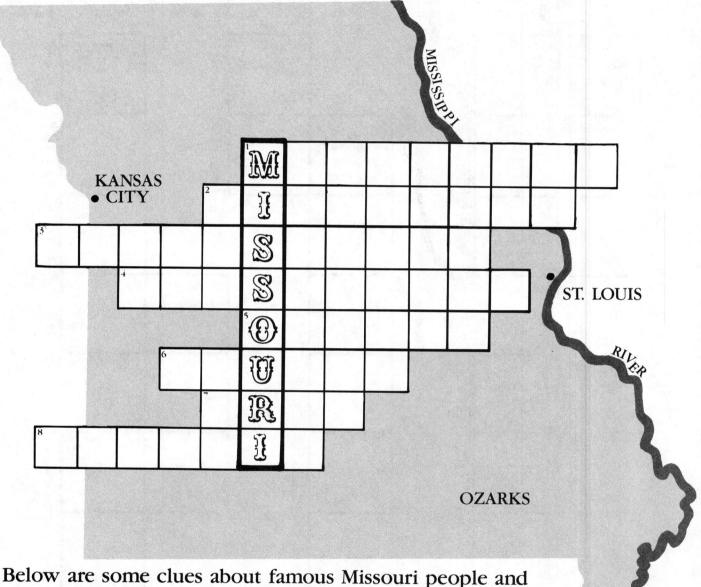

Below are some clues about famous Missouri people and places. Fill in the numbered boxes, going across only. One letter from the word MISSOURI will help you.

1. He wrote the book *The Adventures of Huckleberry Finn*.
2. The Delta Queen is one; it travels the Mississippi River.
3. The river that divides Missouri and Illinois
4. Major city on the western border of the state
5. Vacation area in the southern part of the state with caves, springs, canyons, and lakes
6. Thirty-third president Harry ____ came from Missouri.
7. St. Louis monument called "Gateway to the West"
8. Major city on the eastern border of the state (abbreviated form)

70

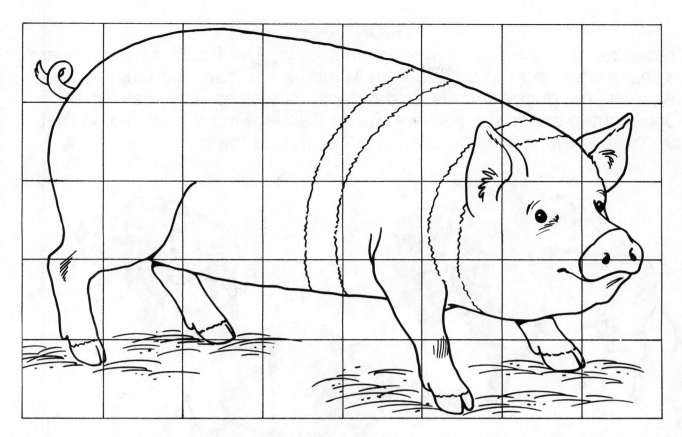

Draw this pig. Look carefully at each square above and draw the same lines in the matching square below. Some lines have been drawn to help you.

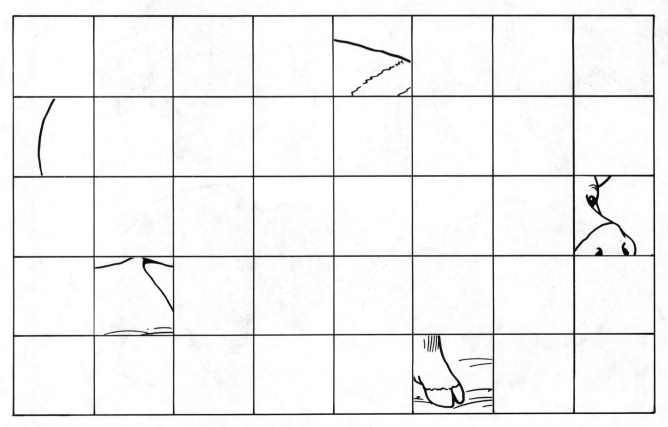

MONTANA

"Montana" is the Spanish word for mountain. The Rocky Mountains are in the western part of the state. In Montana you can visit Indian reservations, dude ranches, and rodeos, as well as hunt, fish, or ski. One sight to see is the National Bison Range. Find the two bison that are exactly the same and draw a circle around them.

Color the picture.

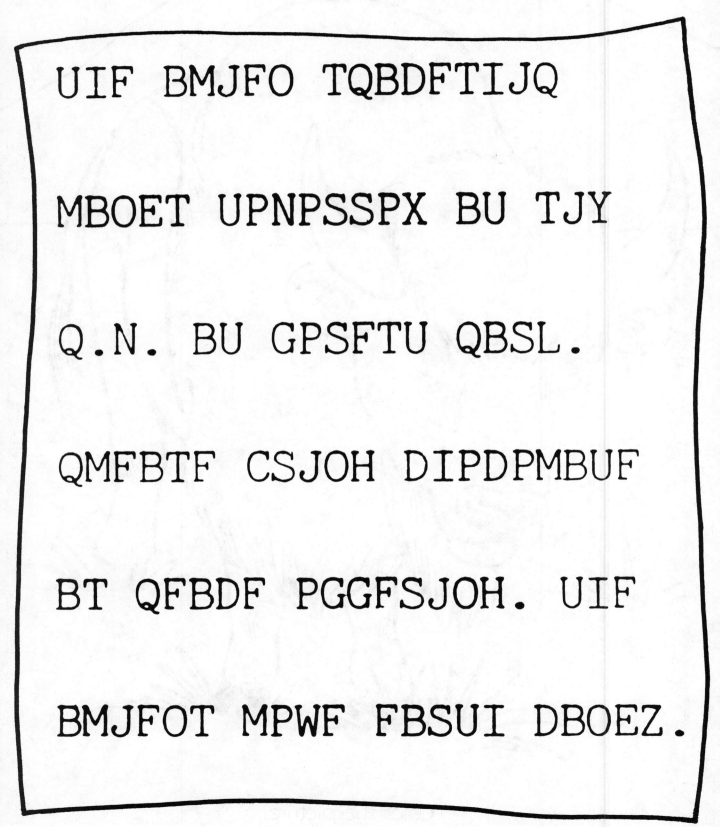

UIF BMJFO TQBDFTIJQ

MBOET UPNPSSPX BU TJY

Q.N. BU GPSFTU QBSL.

QMFBTF CSJOH DIPDPMBUF

BT QFBDF PGGFSJOH. UIF

BMJFOT MPWF FBSUI DBOEZ.

74

NEBRASKA

Nebraska's nickname is the "Cornhusker State." Corn is Nebraska's main crop. Many cornhusking contests used to be held all over the state. Now cornhusking is done by machines.

The pictures below are out of order. Put numbers 1, 2, 3, 4, 5, or 6 in each circle to show the right order.

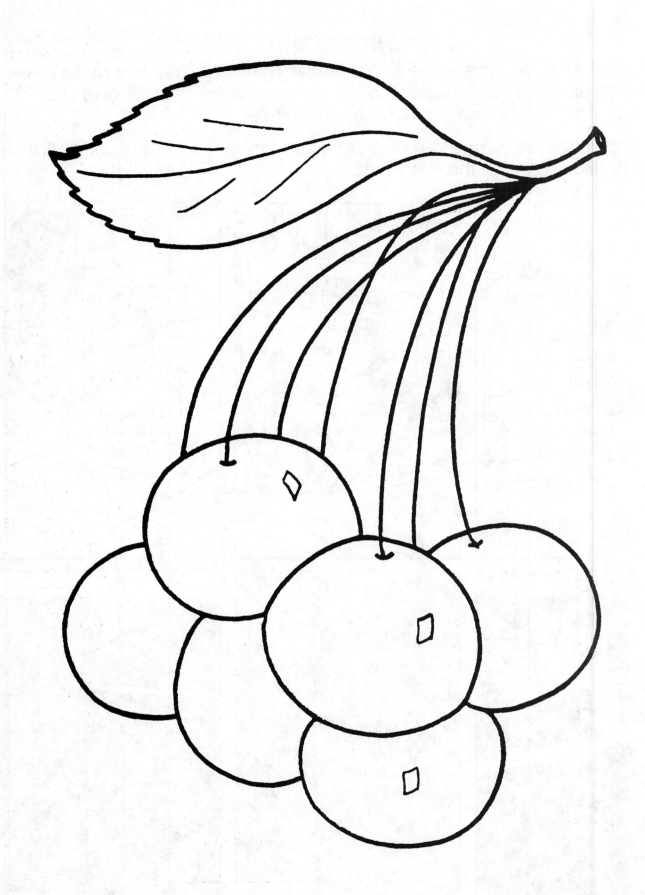

Color the picture.

NEVADA

Las Vegas is the largest city in Nevada. It has many casinos and night clubs. Help Duane Nooton find his way to the Star-Struck Club for his gig tonight. Work quickly—he's late!

NEW HAMPSHIRE

New Hampshire has many mountains. One of the most famous is the Old Man of the Mountain—a 48-foot-high profile of a man's face formed by five granite ledges. If this were a real face, where would the other features be? Draw in his eye, ear, hair, mouth, and anything else you like.

Color the picture.

Tick-tack-toe

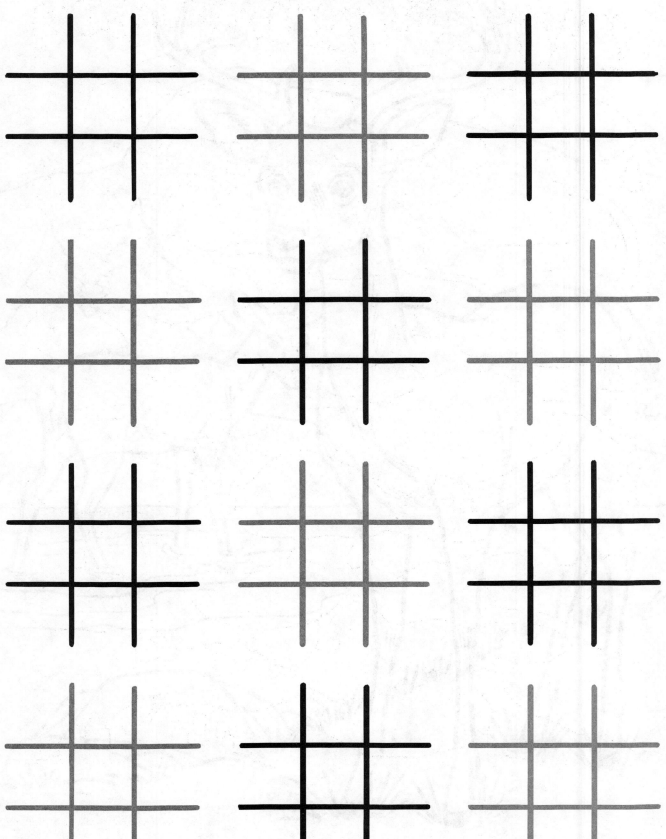

Are you an X, or are you an O? Here's your chance to play tick-tack-toe!

80

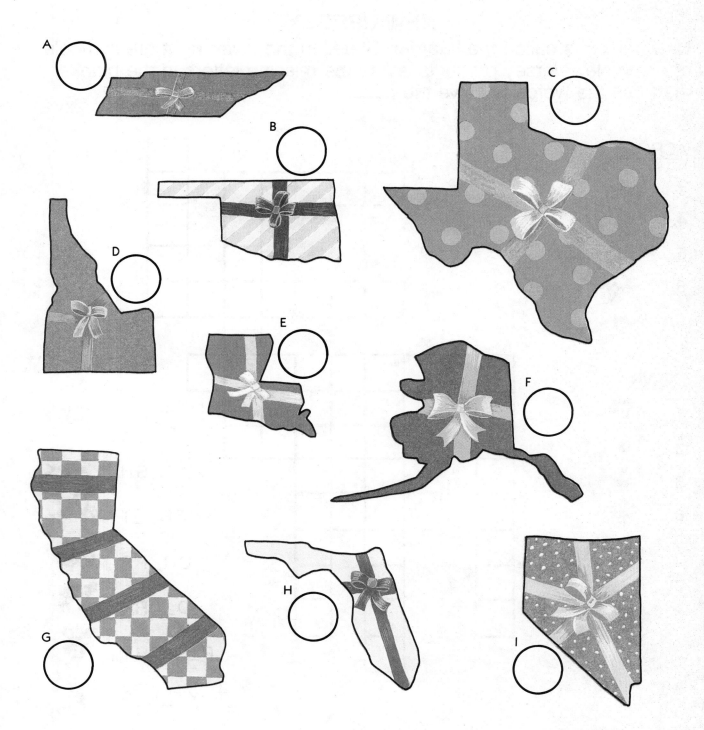

You have been invited to a party—each child is from a different state. Match each kid's home state—wrapped up like a present—with his or her name. Write the correct number in the circles.

1. Maria Miami
2. Judy Juneau
3. Teddy Tulsa
4. Randy Reno
5. Bobby Boise
6. Danny Dallas
7. Newton New Orleans
8. Nancy Nashville
9. Sandy Sacramento

NEW JERSEY

New Jersey is called the "Garden State." In the lower right are symbols of some New Jersey products. Write the missing letters in the blanks, then use the words to solve the puzzle.

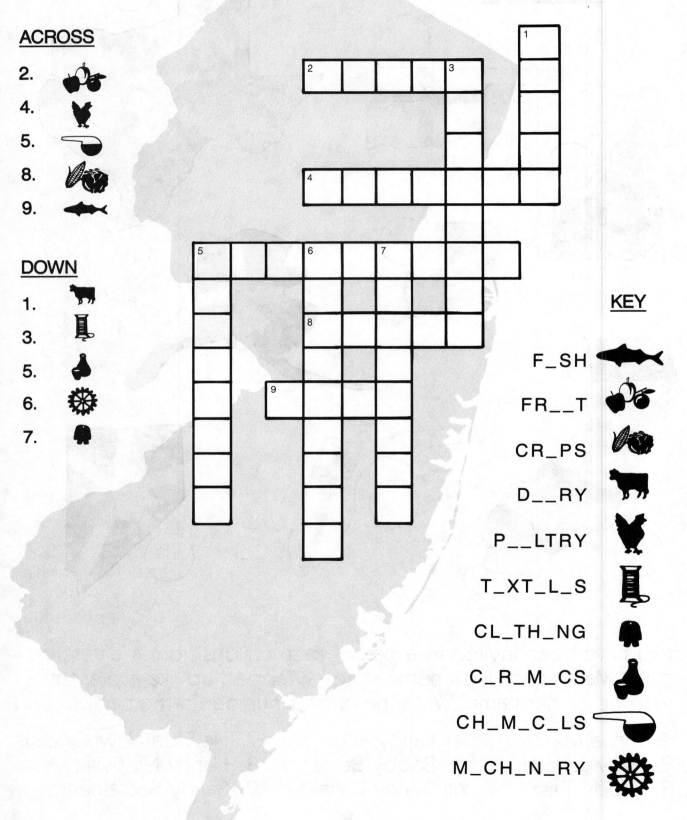

ACROSS

2.

4.

5.

8.

9.

DOWN

1.

3.

5.

6.

7.

KEY

F_SH

FR__T

CR_PS

D__RY

P__LTRY

T_XT_L_S

CL_TH_NG

C_R_M_CS

CH_M_C_LS

M_CH_N_RY

82

Can you get from the triangle at the top to the triangle at the bottom? You can travel only on the lines.

A piece is missing from each of these three things. Look carefully, then circle the piece below that fits.

1 _____

2 _____

3 _____

NEW MEXICO, the "Land of Enchantment"

New Mexico has mountains, forests, deserts, mesas, and the Great Plains. Spanish explorers arrived in the mid-1500s and found Pueblo, Navajo, and Apache Indians living there. The Pueblo Indians built homes of sun-baked brick called "adobe," large enough to house the entire village. The name "Pueblo" means village in Spanish. The Pueblo are peaceful people with their own highly developed civilization.

The Navajo were wanderers who hunted and gathered their food. They built one-room, mud-covered huts called "hogans." The Navajo are well known for their beautiful woven blankets and rugs.

The Apache were brave warriors and, like the Navajo, frequently raided the Pueblo Indians. The Apache built no permanent homes, but lived in brush huts and tepees.

Do you know which Indians lived in each of the dwellings above? Write the name on the line under each picture.

1 _____

NEW YORK
"The Empire State"

New York is one of the largest states on the East Coast. New York City, in the state of New York, has the largest population in the United States. Three of the famous structures shown here are in New York City. Write the name of each landmark on the line provided, then draw a circle around the one that does not belong.

2 _____

3 _____

4 _____

Solve this puzzle by writing these words in the correct spaces above: TOP   MONEY   NUN   DONUT   PEN   TON

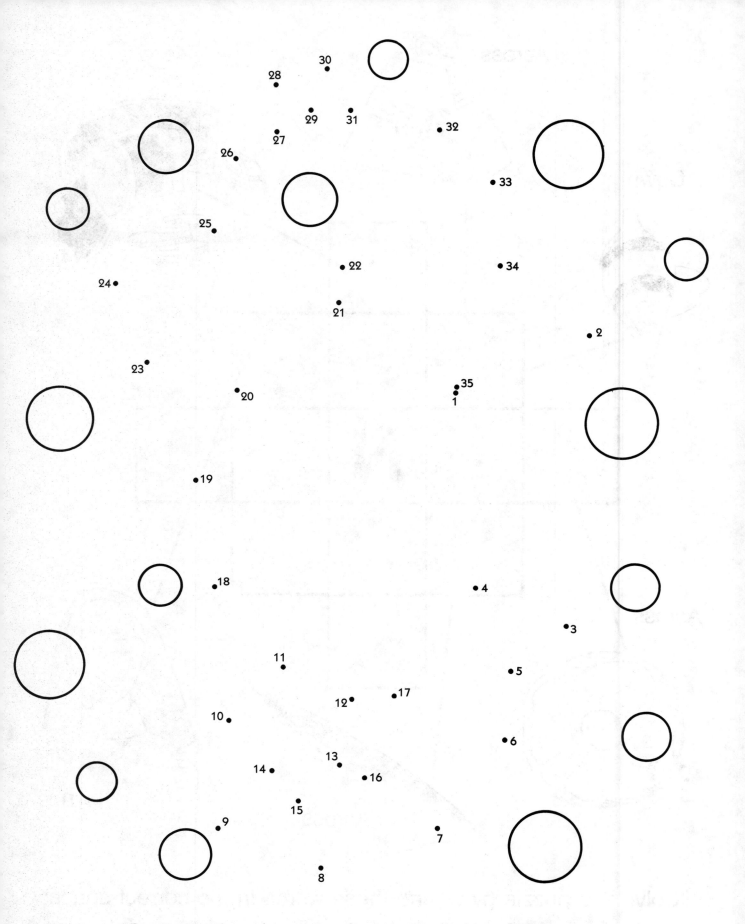

Connect the dots to see what all the circles are.

NORTH CAROLINA

North Carolina has a long coastline on the Atlantic Ocean. Islands, reefs, sandbars, and rough seas make North Carolina's waters very difficult for ships. Because of the many shipwrecks off Cape Hatteras, it has been called the "Graveyard of the Atlantic." Find these hidden treasures in the shipwreck below: a bracelet, coin, fork, eyeglasses, goblet, spoon, and vase.

89

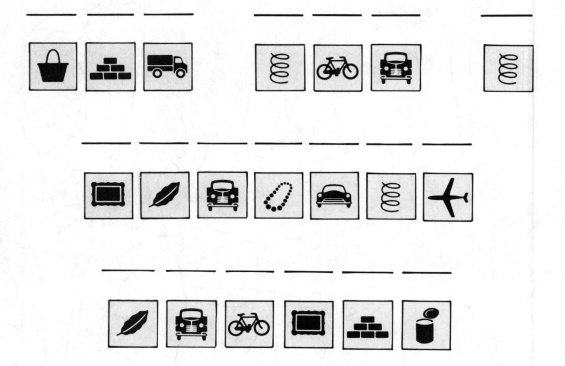

In this code, different pictures stand for different letters of the alphabet. Solve the message above by writing in the blanks the letters that match the pictures.

RiDDlEmaNiA

1. What gets wetter the more it dries?

2. What word is pronounced wrong by even the smartest people?

3. What do elephants have that no other animals have?

4. Why do bees hum?

5. What do you find once in a room, but twice in every corner?

6. What is the best way to start a fire with two sticks?

7. Where can happiness be found?

8. Why did the apple turn over?

9. What did the mayonnaise say when the refrigerator door was open?

10. Six men were under an umbrella. Why didn't any of them get wet?

11. What's the longest word in the dictionary?

12. What has 18 legs and catches flies?

13. What fruit is on a dime?

14. When is a mother like a magician?

15. When is a farmer cruel to his corn?

16. What did the tie say to the hat?

17. What's the hardest thing about learning to ride a bicycle?

18. What is the best thing to put into cookies?

19. What kind of party do snowmen have?

20. What kind of dog has no tail?

21. Why would a spider make a good baseball player?

Connect the dots and then color the picture.

NORTH DAKOTA

Fargo, North Dakota, was named for William G. Fargo. He also gave his name to his stagecoach delivery business — Wells, Fargo & Company, founded in 1852. This stagecoach is going by six hidden pictures. Find a baseball bat, book, frying pan, ice cream cone, pencil, and toothbrush. Then circle them.

Rutherford B. Hayes
Library and Museum.
19th President of U.S.

Oberlin College.
World's first college
to admit women

Akron.
- Rubber Capital
of the United States

• Canton
Go to Football
Hall of Fame

O H I O

Columbus
State Capitol

Cincinnati
see Cincinnati Reds play
at Riverfront
Stadium

Great Serpent Mound
built by Indian tribes several
thousand years ago. It looks
like a snake!

Grand
Rapids   Detroit

South
Bend   Toledo Cleveland
219   419   216   814

ois   513 •Columbus
317   OHIO 614   412
IND.   •Cincinnati
812
ile   Covington   W. VA.

Pam made a map of the places she wanted to visit in Ohio. She tried to get as much information as she could before she left. Pam got a list of phone numbers, but they had no area codes. By using the little map from the phone book, help her figure out the area codes. Note: To find each location, look on the map for the *dot* next to the place name.

Akron Tourist Bureau	_____
Football Hall of Fame	_____
Great Serpent Mound Gift Shop	_____
Hayes Library	_____
Oberlin College	_____
Riverfront Stadium	_____
State Capitol	_____

As you travel along, look around and try to see the things pictured on the bingo cards. As you see each thing, call out its name and then cross it out. The first person to cross out everything in one straight line—down, across, or on a slant—is the winner!

1.

2.

3.

4.

Travel Bingo

Do you know what this animal is? Of "co-rse" you do. It is actually two animals mixed up with each other. What are they? Every other row belongs to the same animal. For example, rows 1 and 3 are parts of one animal. Rows 2 and 4 are parts of the other animal. See if you can identify them.

OKLAHOMA

In the 1820s the United States Government started to move the Creek, Choctaw, Seminole, Chickasaw, and Cherokee Indians to a region west of the Mississippi River. As the white settlers continued to migrate west they took more and more land away from the Indians. Eventually, all the Indians had left was the land that is now the state of Oklahoma.

Pictured here are some things Indians make. There are four of each: baskets, blankets, moccasins, and tepees. In each group there is one that is different from the other three. Put an X on it.

OREGON

This puzzle is about the green and beautiful state of Oregon. Finish each sentence with one of the words given. Hint: match the number of boxes in the puzzle with the number of letters in the word.

ACROSS

2. Oregon's leading industry is ...
   LUMBER TEXTILES FISHING

4. The volcanic mountain that is the highest peak in the state is Mount ...
   JEFFERSON FUJI HOOD

5. Almost half the state of Oregon is covered with ...
   DESERT FOREST WETLANDS

6. The great river that runs along the state's northern border is ...
   DESCHUTES SNAKE COLUMBIA

7. The biggest mountain range in Oregon is the ...
   CASCADE ROCKY APPALACHIAN

DOWN

1. Oregon's state animal is the ...
   BEAVER ELK RACOON

3. The largest city in Oregon is ...
   SALEM EUGENE PORTLAND

Dora Dumm took pictures on her trip, but her aim was not very good. Can you tell what she was trying to take pictures of?

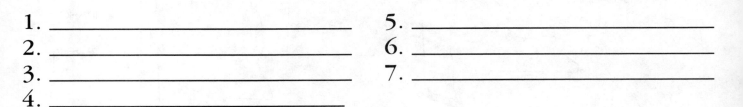

1. _____   5. _____
2. _____   6. _____
3. _____   7. _____
4. _____

Missing: Ten State Capitals

Can you find the state capitals hidden in the sentences below?
Charleston, the capital of West Virginia, appears in the first sentence. It
has been underlined. Find the city in each of the other sentences. Draw a
line under the letters that form the name.

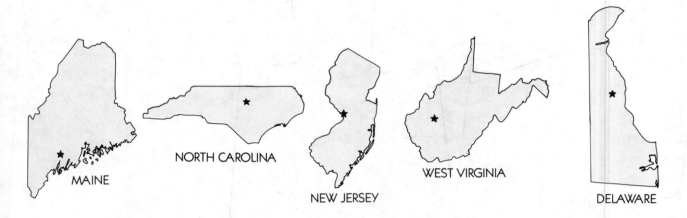

MAINE

NORTH CAROLINA

NEW JERSEY

WEST VIRGINIA

DELAWARE

Tom and Barbie are going to see <u>Charles ton</u>ight.

I hope I do very well in the school play.

Will the carnival ban youngsters from the water slide?

She gave poor Al eight dollars.

Is that a hobo I see in the park?

We harvest our crops in August and September.

My mom treated Jack so nicely.

I get a great rent on my property.

Getting mad is one way to let off steam.

Have you ridden very many horses?

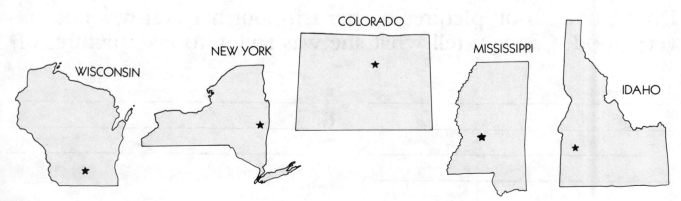

WISCONSIN

NEW YORK

COLORADO

MISSISSIPPI

IDAHO

Find your way through this puzzle by spelling out the five Great Lakes. Begin with the S in Superior and go from letter to letter until you have spelled out the names of all the Great Lakes and finally reach the end with the O in Ontario.

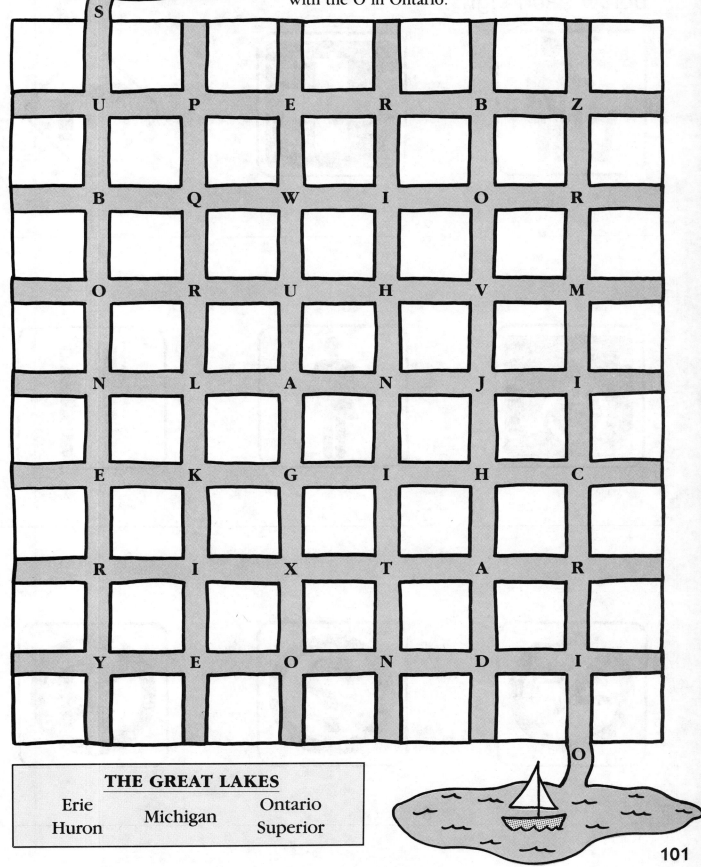

S						
U	P	E	R	B		Z
B	Q	W	I	O		R
O	R	U	H	V		M
N	L	A	N	J		I
E	K	G	I	H		C
R	I	X	T	A		R
Y	E	O	N	D		I
						O

THE GREAT LAKES

Erie		Ontario
Huron	Michigan	Superior

Sign Language

Do you know what these signs mean? Write the answers below each sign.

1. _____   2. _____   3. _____

4. _____   5. _____   6. _____

7. _____   8. _____   9. _____

PENNSYLVANIA

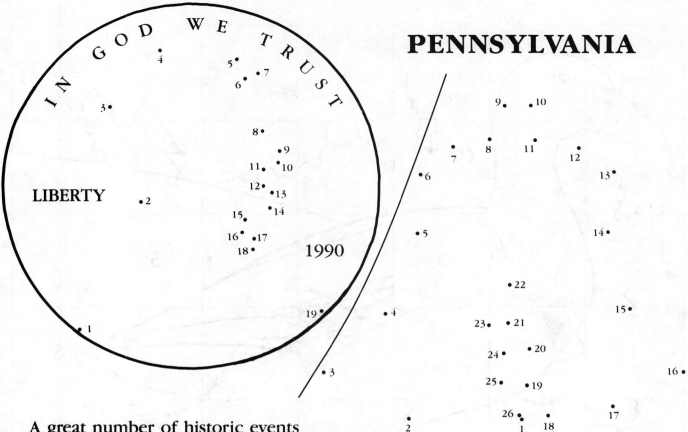

A great number of historic events
have taken place in Pennsylvania.
On July 4, 1776, the Declaration of Independence was adopted at Independence
Hall in Philadelphia. Philadelphia is the state's largest city and was the nation's
capital from 1790 to 1800. The Constitution was also signed there. Pennsylvania
played an important role in the Civil War. The Battle of Gettysburg — a turning
point in the war — was fought there.

Connect the dots in these
pictures to see four things
Pennsylvania is famous for.

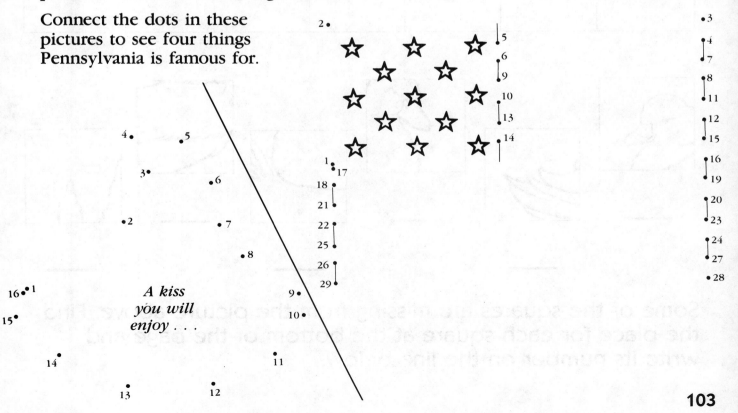

A kiss
you will
enjoy . . .

Some of the squares are missing from the picture above. Find the place for each square at the bottom of the page and write its number on the line below.

RHODE ISLAND
The "Ocean State"

**STATE FLOWER:
VIOLET**

Rhode Island is the smallest of the fifty states. It is also one of the oldest. Providence, the state capital, was the first town to be settled in Rhode Island. Other cities — like Woonsocket and Pawtucket — have Indian names. The famous America's Cup yacht race is often held in Newport. The Newport Jazz Festival is also held there.

Names of some Rhode Island places and features are hidden in the puzzle below. Circle each word as you find it. They are written up, down, across, backwards, and diagonally.

FIND:

**BLOCK ISLAND
FARMING
FISH
JAZZ
NEWPORT
PAWTUCKET
PROVIDENCE
RESORTS
RHODE ISLAND
VIOLET
WESTERLEY
WOONSOCKET
YACHT**

```
E C N E D I V O R P A
R P A W T U C K E T B
Y H T E L O I V E A L
E T O X Q P L K P R O
L H Z D U R C O E T C
R C Z L E O U S T R K
E A A T S I O M Y O I
T Y J N T R S P O P S
S N O R T B W L U W L
E O H S I F Z B A E A
W T E X T I L E S N N
C B A G N I M R A F D
```

SOUTH CAROLINA

Pirates sailed along the coast of South Carolina in the 1700s, attacking and plundering other ships. If they were caught, pirates were hanged on Charleston's execution dock. One of the most famous pirates who terrorized the Charleston coast was Captain Edward Teach, known as "Blackbeard." In each row of pictures below, circle the two that are exactly alike.

Color the picture.

SOUTH DAKOTA

Mount Rushmore National Memorial, in South Dakota, is a sculpture of four great United States Presidents carved right out of a cliff. The artist, Gutzon Borghum, worked on the 60-foot-high sculpture from 1925 until his death in 1941. Mount Rushmore honors Presidents Washington, Jefferson, Lincoln, and one more. Do you know who he is? There are four possibilities below, with their names scrambled. Unscramble the names, then circle the name of the President that really does appear on Mount Rushmore.

DEENKYN

1 _____

AGARNE

2 _____

SOOVELERT

3 _____

KLIFARNN

4 _____

6		8
7	5	3
		4

MAGIC NUMBER 15

If you study the number square at left, you will find that the numbers have been arranged so that they add up to 15 up, down, across, and diagonally. Write in the missing numbers.

Now try this magic number square. Use the numbers 1, 2, 3, 4, 5, 6, 7, 8, and 9 only once in the squares so they add up to 15 up, down, across, and diagonally.

	3	
1		9
6		

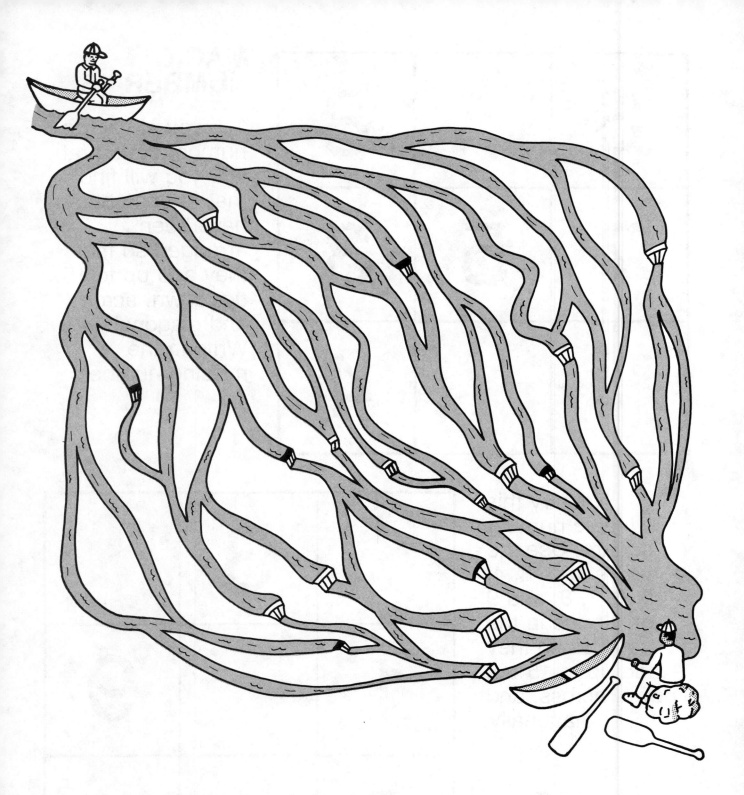

Dams are built to control floods, to make rivers deeper, and to provide electric power. There are many dams in and around Tennessee. Joe is in the top left corner. Help him to reach his friend Bob. Joe can go in any direction on a river, but he cannot go over a dam.

Look at these silhouettes.
Count how many things you can
find that start with the letter "T."

Play this game with a friend. Write an X in any box.
Have your friend write an O in any other box. Keep taking turns writing X's and O's. The first one to get five X's or O's in a line in any direction (up, down, across, or diagonally) wins.

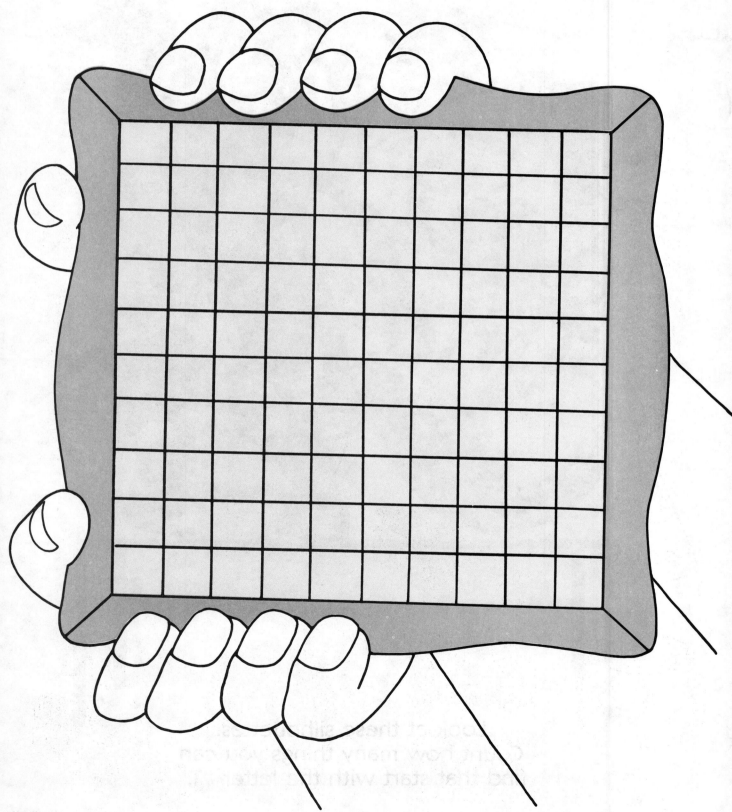

"I WENT ON A TRIP AND I PACKED ..."

Here's a game the whole family can play in the car. The first player says, "I went on a trip and I packed ..." and then names something that begins with the letter A, like an atlas. The next player says, "I went on a trip and I packed an atlas and a ..." and then names something that starts with B, like a beachball. Each player has to repeat the objects already named, then add a word that begins with the next letter of the alphabet. So the third player might say, "I went on a trip and I packed an atlas, a beachball, and a cat." You can pack anything you want — sensible or silly. Play until you have gone through the whole alphabet.

Play this memory teaser by yourself or with other players. Using the categories along the top, fill in the boxes below with words starting with the letters in the left-hand column. The first line has been done to help you get started.

	Boy's or Girl's Name	City or State	Performer or Rock Group
T	TAMMY	TEXAS	TIFFANY
R			
A			
V			
E			
L			
F			
U			
N			

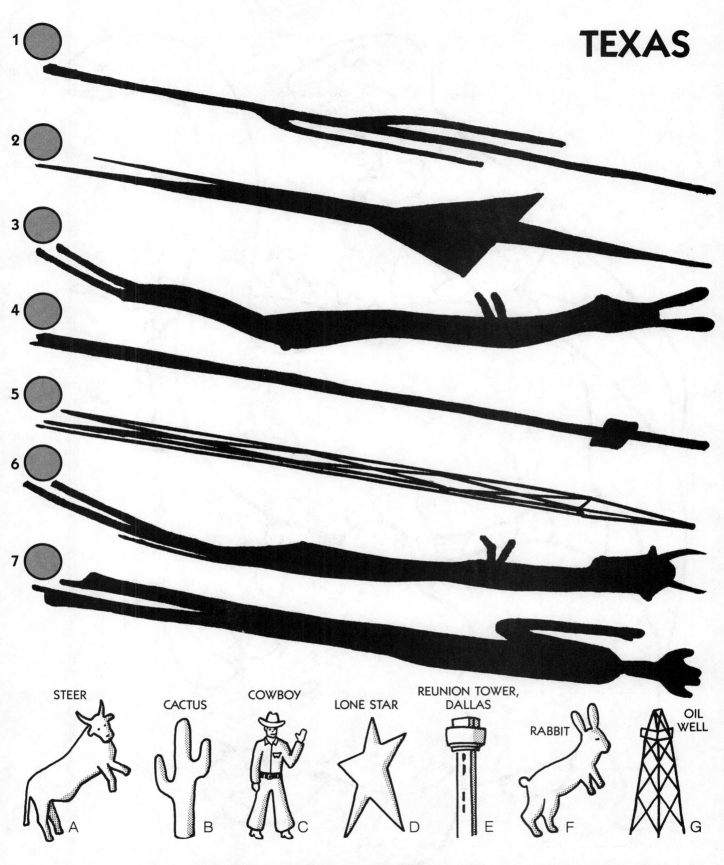

1

2

3

4

5

6

7

STEER

A

CACTUS

B

COWBOY

C

LONE STAR

D

REUNION TOWER, DALLAS

E

RABBIT

F

OIL WELL

G

Texas is a very big state. It is sunny and has wide open spaces where you can cast a *long* shadow. Match these Texas sights at the bottom of the page with their shadows above. Then write the object's letter in its circle.

Color the picture.

UTAH

Lots of dinosaur fossils have been found in Utah. You can see many of them at the Dinosaur National Monument.

Look at the dinosaur pictures above and circle the one in each section that is different from the others.

A CAVERN TO COLOR

This big limestone cavern beneath the earth's surface was made when surface water seeped into cracks in the limestone. Over time the water gradually widened the cracks and underground streams formed. The water underground made passages and, eventually, caves. Over thousands of years dripping water inside the caves formed deposits called stalactites and stalagmites. Carlsbad Caverns in New Mexico is the largest system of caverns in the world. It's easy to remember which deposits are stalactites and which are stalagmites: Stalactites have a "c" and they hang from the ceiling.

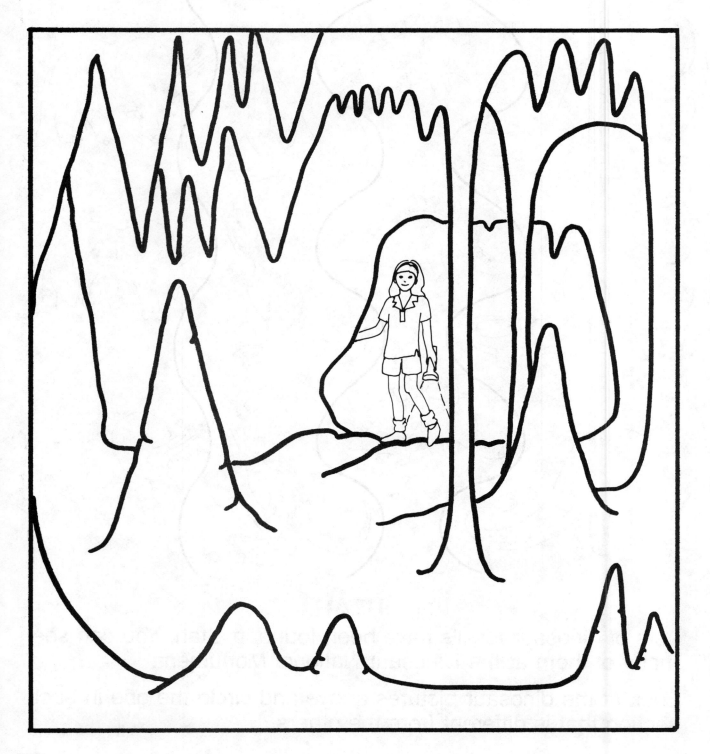

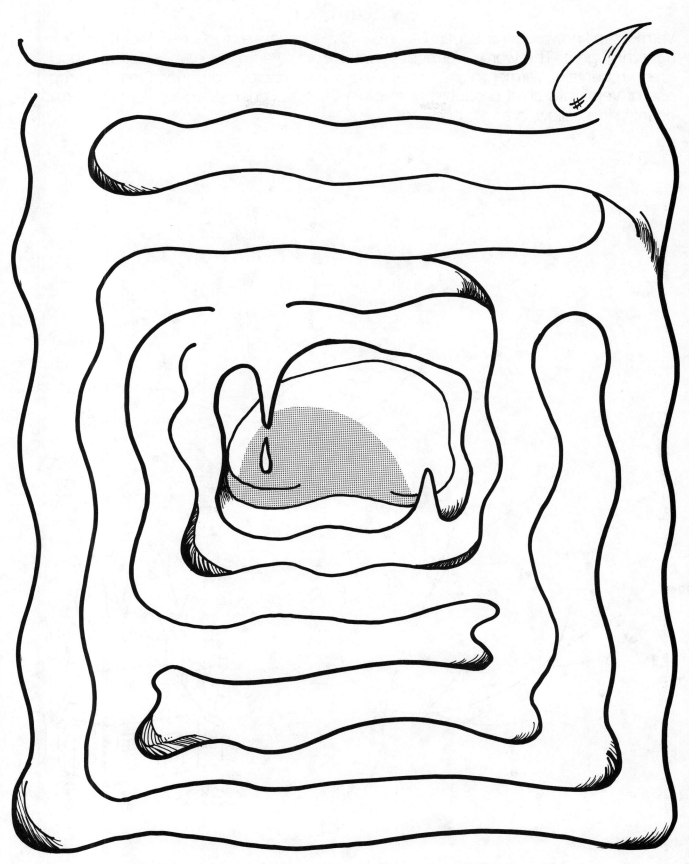

It takes thousands of years for water to seep down through limestone rocks and form caves. Use your pencil or crayon to find
which way the water has seeped to make this cave.

VERMONT

Vermont is known as the Green Mountain State because the Green Mountains run right through it. The word "Vermont" comes from "vert mont," which is French for green mountain. Vermont's state tree is the sugar maple. It produces maple syrup, one of Vermont's chief products. In autumn the trees change colors, turning Vermont's countryside yellow, orange, and red.

First connect the numbered dots, then the lettered dots. Color the picture in autumn colors.

Fit the different state names into this puzzle by counting the number of letters in each word and figuring out where they fit. One is done to help you get started.

4 Letters	5 Letters	6 Letters	7 Letters
IOWA	IDAHO	HAWAII	ALABAMA
OHIO	MAINE	KANSAS	ARIZONA
UTAH	TEXAS	NEVADA	FLORIDA
		OREGON	GEORGIA
			INDIANA
			MONTANA
			NEW YORK
			✔ VERMONT
			WYOMING

This picture is made of many different shapes. How many of the following shapes can you find?

squares _____

circles _____

triangles _____

rectangles _____

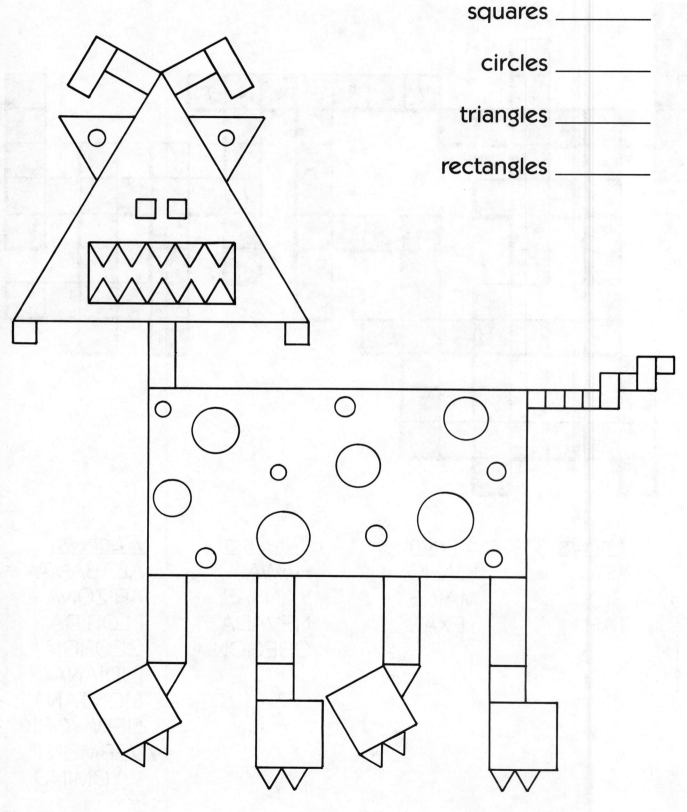

1 PJREAMSES MIONDREONET

2 PJORHESN ITDYENLETR

3 PWORODEROSW WIIDLESONNT

4 ZPACRHEARSY ITADYENLOTR

5 PJRAEMSES IMADDIESNONT

6 TPHORMAESS IJEDFFEERNSOTN

7 WPILRLIAEM SHEINRDY HEARNRISTON

8 PGEROREGSEI WADSHIENNGTTON

VIRGINIA

Virginia has been nicknamed ''Mother of Presidents'' because more Presidents have been born there than in any other state. To find out which Presidents were born in Virginia, cross out the letters P, R, E, S, I, D, E, N, T below each statue.

The shapes below contain a hidden picture. To find it, first solve each math equation. Then follow these simple instructions to finish the picture:

Color each equation shape equaling 6 green.
Color each equation shape equaling 7 blue.
Color each equation shape equaling 8 brown.
Color each equation shape equaling 9 yellow.
Color each equation shape equaling 10 orange.

124

WASHINGTON

Washington is on the Pacific Coast, in the northwestern corner of the United States mainland. Washington has large forests of hemlock, pine, fir, spruce, and cedar and is a leading producer of pulp, plywood, and other wood products. We can help preserve these beautiful forests by using recycled paper products whenever possible. Draw a circle around the things made from wood or paper.

Washington, D.C.

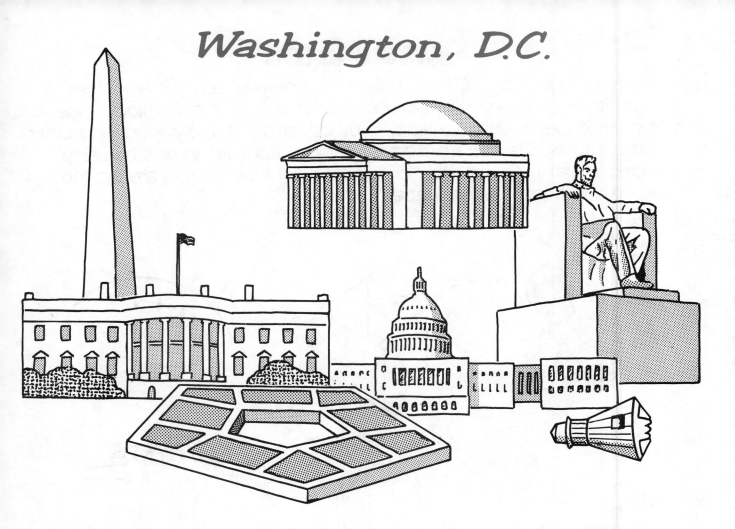

Washington, D.C. is the capital of the United States. Jan went there on vacation and saw many famous buildings. She saw the Washington Monument which is the tallest structure in the city. She visited the Jefferson Memorial and the Lincoln Memorial. She went to the White House (where the President lives) and to the Pentagon, headquarters for the Department of Defense. Other places she saw were the Capitol Building — where the members of Congress meet — and the Air and Space Museum.

Jan made a collage from pictures of her favorite sights. Now she wants to frame her collage. Circle the frame below that fits.

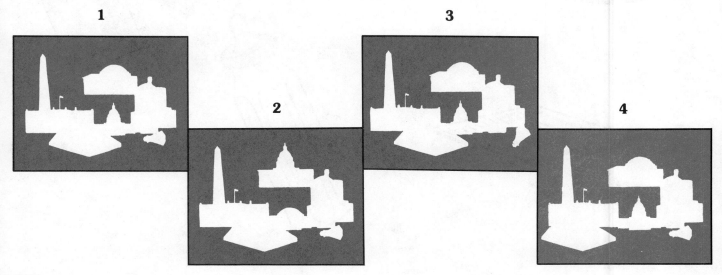

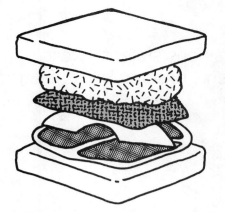

Whachamacallit

Doodad

Doohickey

Thingamabob

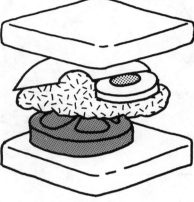

Whoosis

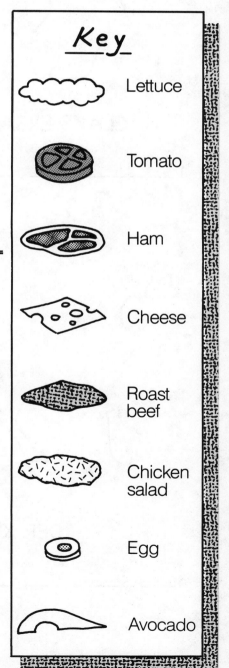

The Hungertons stopped at the sandwich shop for lunch. Help them decide what to order.

1. Harvey wants something with ham and cheese. What is the best sandwich for him?

2. Hedda is a vegetarian. Which sandwich should she order?

3. Hannah can't eat eggs but definitely wants avocado. What should she get?

4. Harry and Hank want to split a sandwich, but Harry doesn't like roast beef and Hank doesn't like cheese. Which sandwich should they get?

5. Helen wants tomato on her sandwich but no chicken salad or egg. What sandwich should she order?

WEST VIRGINIA

Many kinds of animals live in the beautiful, mountainous state of West Virginia. To find some of them, connect the dots and unscramble the letters.

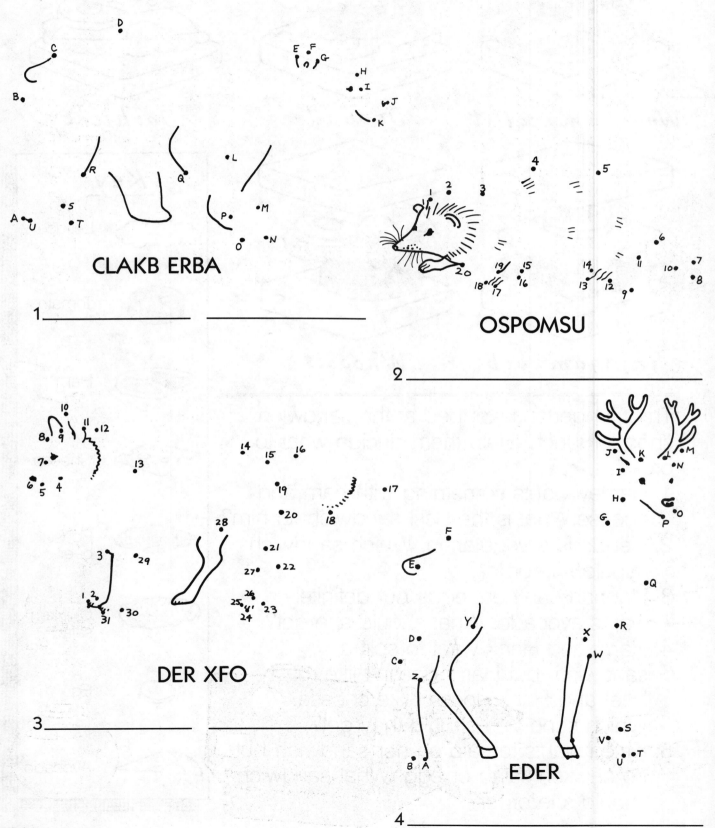

CLAKB ERBA

1 _____ _____

OSPOMSU

2 _____

DER XFO

3 _____ _____

EDER

4 _____

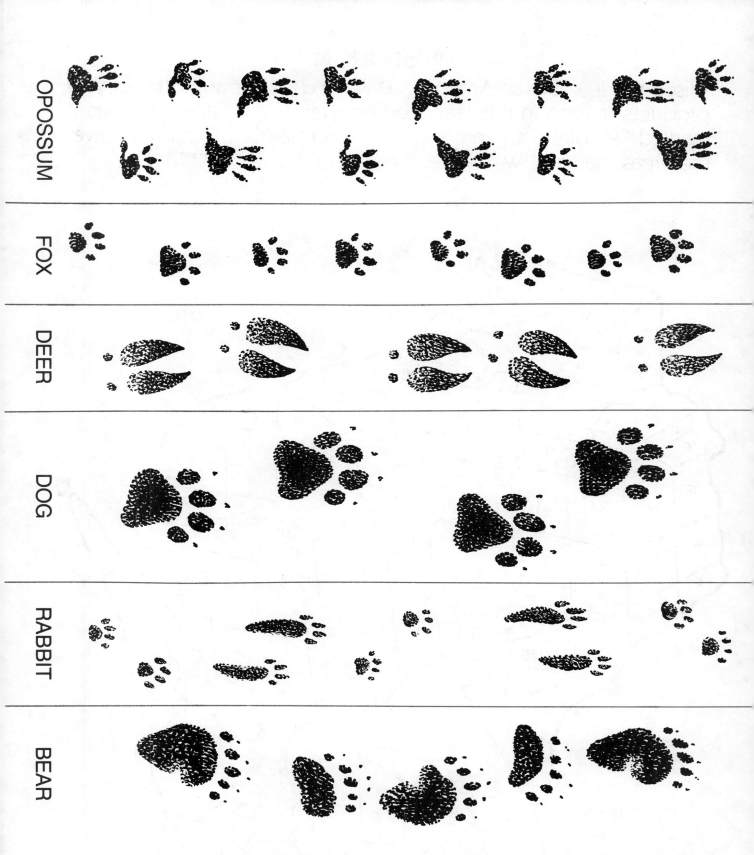

OPOSSUM

FOX

DEER

DOG

RABBIT

BEAR

Have you ever seen tracks on the ground in the woods or park? The pattern made by an animal's footprints is called a "trail." The next time you go on a hike, you can take this page with you to help identify the kind of animal that walked there before you.

WISCONSIN

Wisconsin is know as America's Dairyland. There are four dairy products hidden in the map. To find them, color all the shapes marked "P" pink, "O" orange, "G" green, and "Y" yellow. Leave the areas marked "W" white.

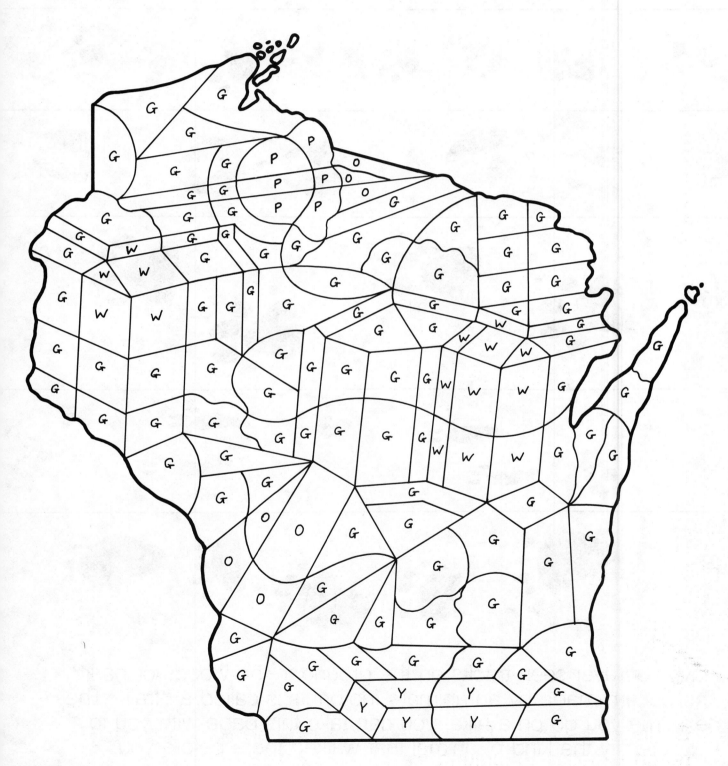

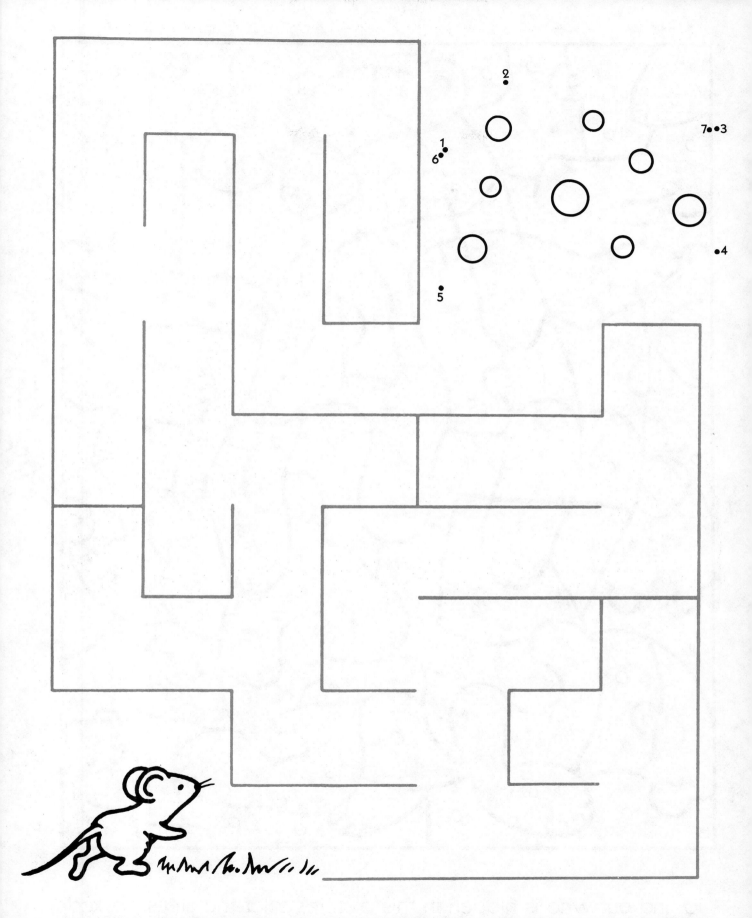

Connect the dots. Then help the mouse through the maze to reach what he is looking for.

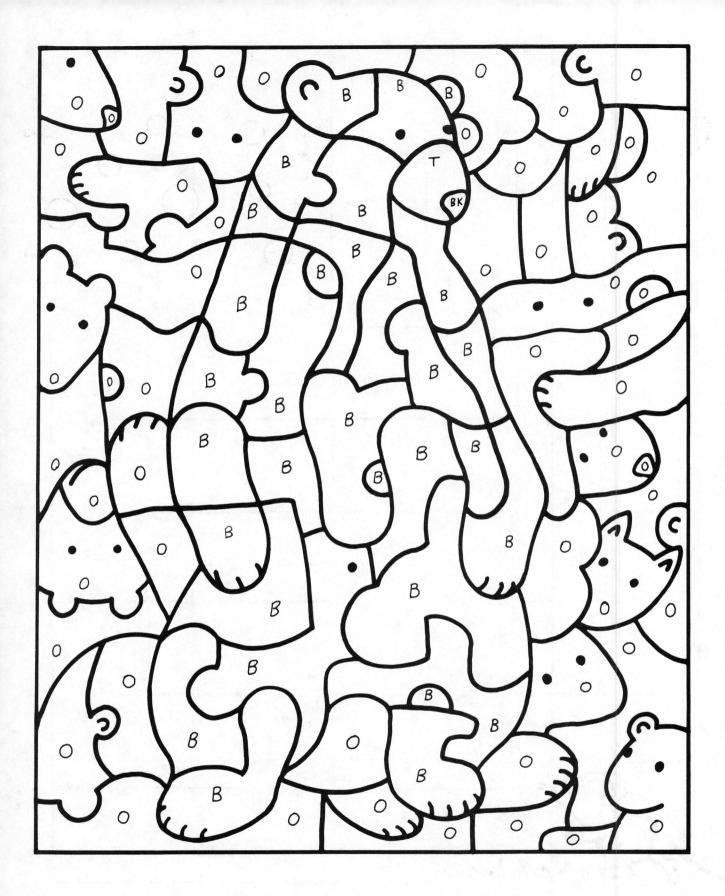

To find out who is hidden in this picture, color the areas marked "B" brown, "BK" black, "T" tan, and "O" any color you like.

WYOMING

Yellowstone National Park in Wyoming was established as America's first national park in 1872. Each year millions of visitors enjoy the park's natural beauty.

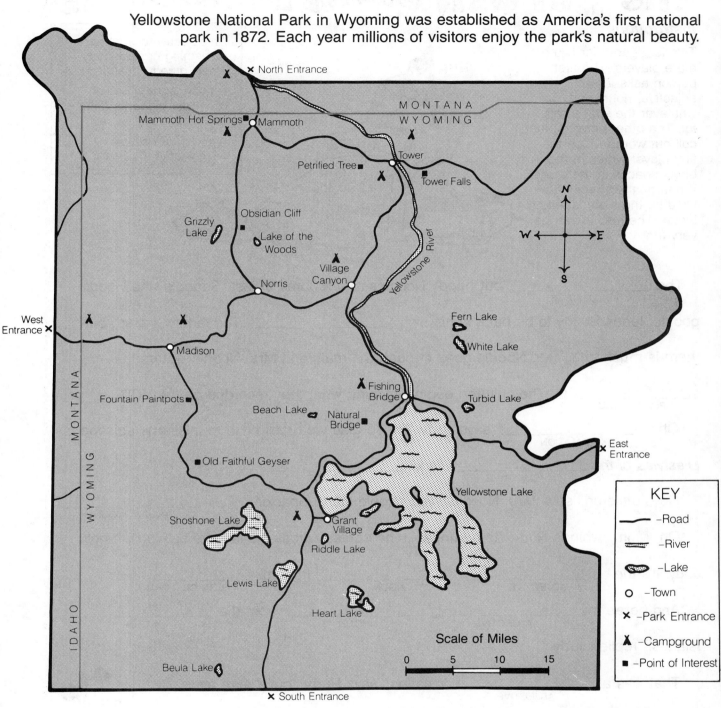

Look at this map of Yellowstone National Park. Then use the key to answer these questions:

1. Which park entrance is the farthest from a campground?
2. Which towns would you pass through if you drove from the west entrance of the park to Fishing Bridge if you took the road that runs along the river? If you took the route that goes along the lake?
3. Which town is near the most lakes?
4. About how many miles are between Mammoth and Tower? Between Grant Village and Beula Lake?
5. What direction is Yellowstone Lake from Old Faithful Geyser?
6. Which town is close to a lake, a river, and a campground?

The RETURN of the NOODLES

Instructions

This is a game for two or more players. The first person asks for an adjective, noun, verb or whatever the space calls for. The other player(s) then call out words which the first player writes in the blank spaces in the story. When all the spaces are filled in, the story is read aloud. The results can be very funny.

An adjective describes something or somebody— small, greedy, beautiful.

A noun is the name of a person, place, or thing— car, elbow, boy.

A verb is an action word—jump, fly, throw.

The _____ but happy Noodles return home at last. Stroodle, the Noodle
       ADJECTIVE

poodle, leaps for joy to be back in his own _____. The family is tired, but
                                              NOUN

there is much to do. Mr. Noodle goes through the mail, and Mrs. Noodle waters the

_____. The children begin watching what they recorded on the VCR.
PLURAL NOUN

"Oh, _____!" says Judy. "I'm so glad we didn't have to miss one episode of
      EXCLAMATION

Lifestyles of the _____ *and* _____!"
                    ADJECTIVE   ADJECTIVE

"Now, children," says Mrs. Noodle, "you should start unpacking your _____."
                                                                     PLURAL NOUN

"Oh, Mom," whines Rudy. As he unpacks he comes across his favorite souvenir. "Look,

Judy. It's the _____ _____ I got in _____!"
                ADJECTIVE   NOUN   CITY OR TOWN

"And here's my _____ _____ from the _____
                ADJECTIVE   NOUN   NOUN

Islands!" replies Judy.

"That was a _____ vacation," says Rudy, "but it sure feels
             ADJECTIVE

_____ to be back home."
ADJECTIVE

Whodunit?

Look at the scene of the crimes above. Then look at the suspects below to find the culprits.

1. Who ate the banana?
2. Who took a snack from the refrigerator?
3. Who was looking in the cupboard?
4. Who broke the window?
5. Who got into the cookie jar?

Fran	Jean	Jimmy	Shrimpy	Falona
"Freckleface"	"The Bean"	"The Gerbil"	"The Shrimp"	"Baloney"
Franklin	McClean	Johnson	Shrimpton	Maloney

Look through the whole book carefully and when you find the matching picture, write the page number in the given space.

ANSWERS

Page 4

ALE	EAT	REAL
ARE	ERA	TALE
ART	LATE	TAR
AT	LATER	TEA
ATE	LET	TEAR
AVERT	RAT	VALE
EAR	RATE	VAT
EARL	RAVE	VEAL
		VET

... And many more!

Page 5

B-6	Bird Eye
E-6	Friendship
F-9	Bald Hill
B-1	Zip City
D-5	Mars Hill
A-8	Tibbie

Hatchechubbee	G-6
Gum Springs	D-3
Dog Town	F-2
Deposit	D-1
Six Mile	C-5
Josephine	C-10

Page 6

A,4 ; B,1 ; C,3 ; D,2 ; E,5.

Page 7

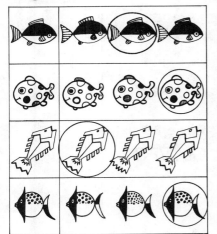

Page 9

Page 11

1, 3, 5, 7, **9**
2, 5, 8, 11, **14**
12, 11, 10, 9, **8**
1, 2, 4, 8, **16**
18, 15, 12, 9, **6**

Page 13

We like Arkansas because of:

Little Rock
Mystic Cavern
Crater of Diamonds
Sugarloaf Mountain

Page 14

1. Berkeley
2. San Francisco
3. San Jose
4. Oakland
5. Monterey
6. Fresno
7. Pasadena
8. Santa Barbara
9. Los Angeles
10. Anaheim
11. San Diego

Page 15

Answers will vary.

Page 17

Page 18

Page 19

Page 21

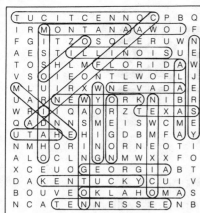

Page 22

Lady's Slipper
Trumpet Vine
Violet
Honeysuckle
Crocus

Page 27

Answers will vary.

Page 29

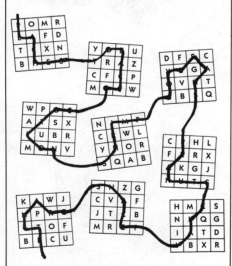

Page 31

1. Go up Apple Avenue, turn left on Parsley Path, and go straight ahead to Pineapple Upside-Down ride on Raspberry Road.
2. The closest restroom is on Raspberry Road.
3. They should get off at Stop A.
4. Billy arrives at the Bumper Bananas first.

Page 32

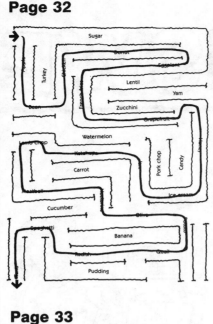

Page 33

Page 34

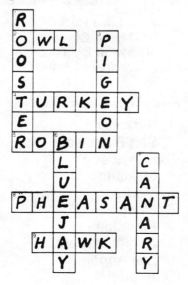

Page 36

Page 37

Page 38

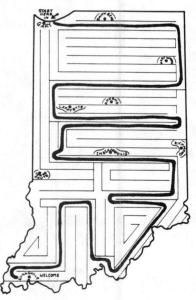

Page 39

GLOVES

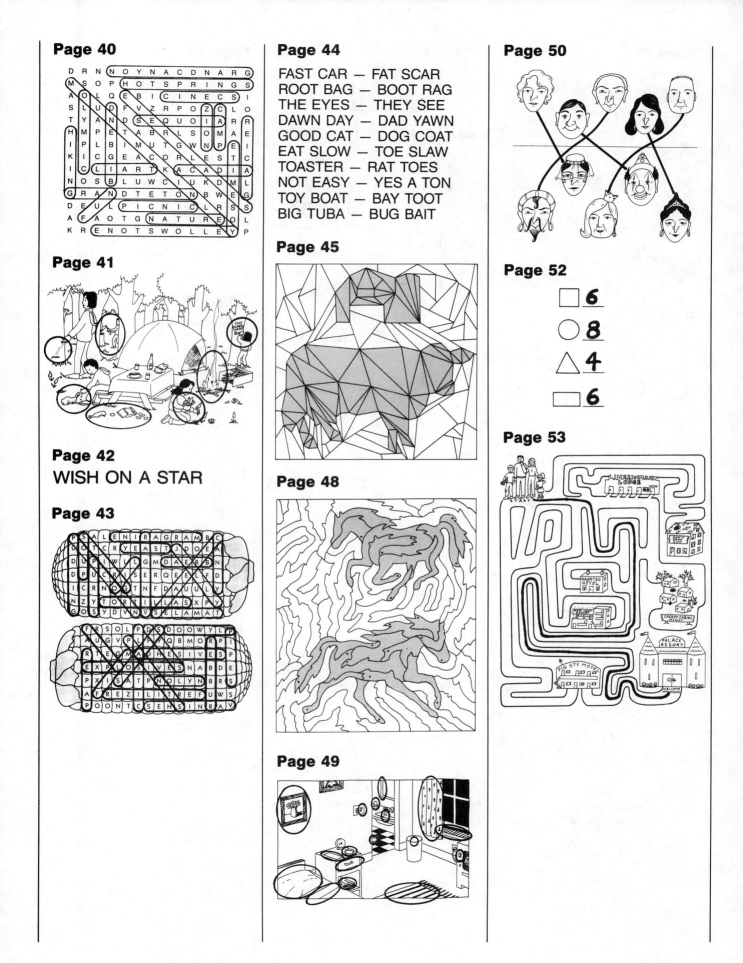

Page 40

Page 41

Page 42

WISH ON A STAR

Page 43

Page 44

FAST CAR — FAT SCAR
ROOT BAG — BOOT RAG
THE EYES — THEY SEE
DAWN DAY — DAD YAWN
GOOD CAT — DOG COAT
EAT SLOW — TOE SLAW
TOASTER — RAT TOES
NOT EASY — YES A TON
TOY BOAT — BAY TOOT
BIG TUBA — BUG BAIT

Page 45

Page 48

Page 49

Page 50

Page 52

□ 6
○ 8
△ 4
□ 6

Page 53

Page 56

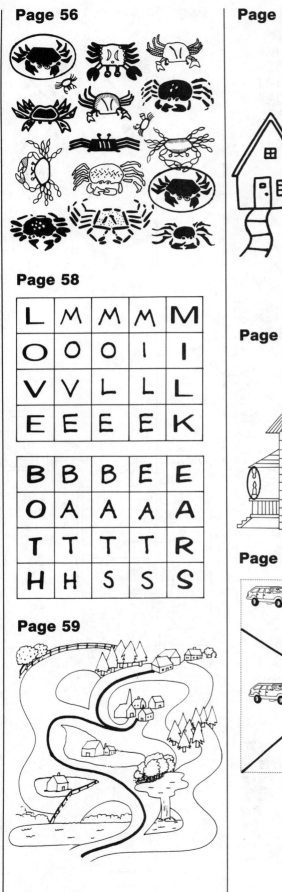

Page 58

L	M	M	M	M
O	O	O	I	I
V	V	L	L	L
E	E	E	E	K

B	B	B	E	E
O	A	A	A	A
T	T	T	T	R
H	H	S	S	S

Page 59

Page 60

Page 61

Page 62

Page 63

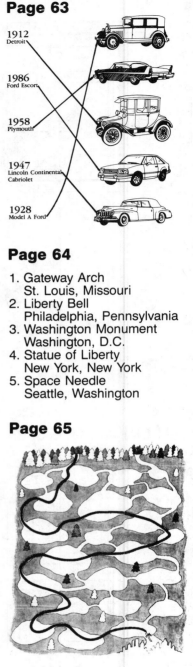

1912
Detroit

1986
Ford Escort

1958
Plymouth

1947
Lincoln Continental
Cabriolet

1928
Model A Ford

Page 64

1. Gateway Arch
   St. Louis, Missouri
2. Liberty Bell
   Philadelphia, Pennsylvania
3. Washington Monument
   Washington, D.C.
4. Statue of Liberty
   New York, New York
5. Space Needle
   Seattle, Washington

Page 65

Page 66

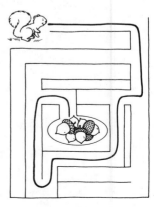

Page 67

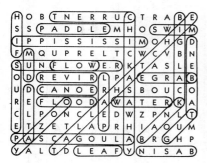

Page 70

```
        M A R K T W A I N
        R I V E R B O A T
M I S S I S S I P P I
    K A N S A S C I T Y
              O Z A R K S
          T R U M A N
              A R C H
S T L O U I S
```

Page 72

Page 74

THE ALIEN SPACESHIP
LANDS TOMORROW AT SIX
P.M. AT FOREST PARK.
PLEASE BRING CHOCOLATE
AS PEACE OFFERING. THE
ALIENS LOVE EARTH CANDY.

Page 75

Page 77

Page 81

A,8 ; B,3 ; C,6 ; D,5 ; E,7 ;
F,2 ; G,9 ; H,1 ; I,4.

Page 82

```
                    D
        F R U I T   A
              E     I
              X     R
        P O U L T R Y
              I
  C H E M I C A L S
  E       A     E
  R       C R O P S
  A       H   T
  M     F I S H I N G
  I       N   I
  C       E   N
  S       R   G
          Y
```

Page 83

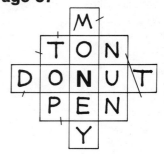

Page 84

Page 85

1. Pueblo
2. Navajo
3. Apache

Page 86

1. Brooklyn Bridge
2. Statue of Liberty
3. Empire State Building
4. Lincoln Memorial

The Lincoln Memorial is not in
New York City. It is in
Washington, D.C.

Page 87

```
          M
    T O   N
D O N E T
    P   U N
    E   N
    Y
```

Page 89

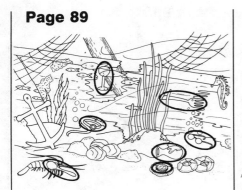

Page 90

YOU ARE A
SPECIAL
PERSON

Page 91

1. A towel
2. Wrong
3. Baby elephants
4. Because they don't know the words
5. The letter "r"
6. Make sure one of them is a match.
7. In the dictionary
8. Because it saw the jelly roll
9. "Shut the door. I'm dressing."
10. It wasn't raining.
11. Smiles. There's a mile between the first and last letter.
12. A baseball team
13. A date
14. When she turns the car into a driveway
15. At harvest time, when he has to pull its ears
16. "You go on ahead. I'll hang around."
17. The ground
18. Your teeth
19. A snow ball
20. A hot dog
21. Because it is good at catching flies

Page 93

Page 94

Akron Tourist Bureau   216
Football Hall of Fame   216
Great Serpent Mound Gift Shop 513
Hayes Library   419
Oberlin College   216
Riverfront Stadium   513
State Capitol   614

Page 96

Counting from the top, the even numbered rows show a cow. The odd numbered rows show a horse.

Page 97

Page 98

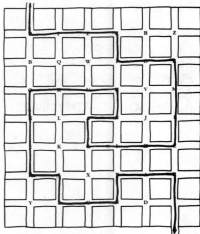

Page 99

1. An elephant
2. High-heeled shoes
3. A telephone
4. A swimming fish
5. Someone throwing a football
6. Mountains and sky
7. The Statue of Liberty

Page 100

I hope I **do ver**y well in the school play. (Delaware)
Will the carniv**al ban y**oungsters from the water slide? (New York)
She gave poo**r Al eigh**t dollars. (North Carolina)
Is that a ho**bo I se**e in the park? (Idaho)
We harvest our crops in **August and** September. (Maine)
My mom treated **Jack so n**icely. (Mississippi)
I get a grea**t rent on** my property. (New Jersey)
Getting **mad is on**e way of getting even. (Wisconsin)
Have you rid**den ver**y many horses? (Colorado)

Page 101

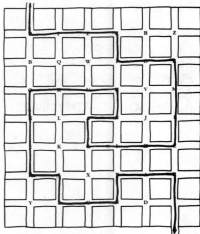

Page 102

1. Put trash here
2. Hospital
3. Left turn
4. Wheelchair access
5. Women's restroom
6. Restaurant
7. No smoking
8. Information
9. No parking

Page 103

A penny made at the United States Mint in Philadelphia, the Liberty Bell, a chocolate kiss from Hershey, PA, the first American flag sewn by Betsy Ross

Page 104

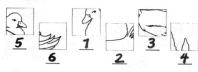

Page 105

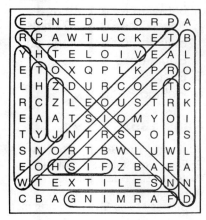

Page 106

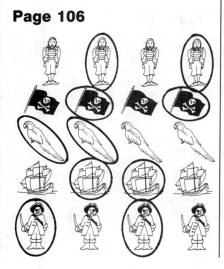

Page 108

1. KENNEDY
2. REAGAN
3. ROOSEVELT
4. FRANKLIN

Theodore Roosevelt is on Mount Rushmore.

Page 109

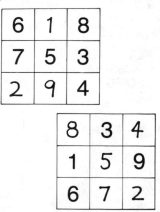

Page 110

Page 111

Table	Toad	Tricycle
Telephone	Top	Truck
Television	Tooth	Trumpet
Tent	Toothbrush	Tulip
Tepee	Toucan	Turkey
Texas	Tree	Turnip
Tie	Triangle	Turtle

Page 114

Answers will vary.

Page 115

1,B ; 2,D ; 3,F ; 4,E ; 5,G ; 6,A ; 7,C.

Page 117

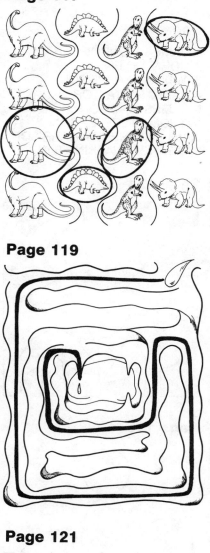

Page 119

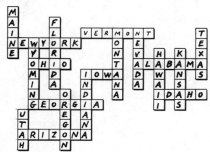

Page 121

(crossword puzzle of U.S. states)

Page 122

Page 123

1. JAMES MONROE
2. JOHN TYLER
3. WOODROW WILSON
4. JACHARY TAYLOR
5. JAMES MADISON
6. THOMAS JEFFERSON
7. WILLIAM HENRY HARRISON
8. GEORGE WASHINGTON

Page 124

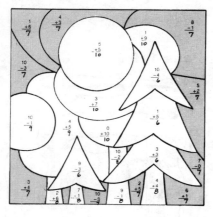

Page 125

Page 126

Frame 1 fits the collage.

Page 127

1. Doodad
2. Doohickey
3. Whachamacallit
4. Whoosis
5. Doodad

Page 128

1. BLACK BEAR
2. OPOSSUM
3. RED FOX
4. DEER

Page 130

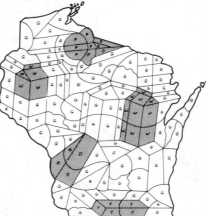

Page 131

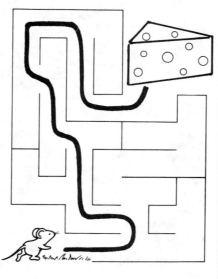

Page 132

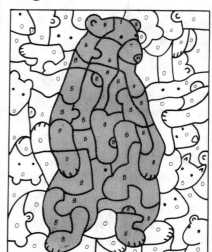

Page 133

1. The East Entrance
2. River route: Madison, Norris, Village Canyon
   Lake route: Madison
3. Grant Village
4. There are 15 miles between Mammoth and Tower. There are 20 miles between Grant Village and Beula Lake.
5. East
6. Fishing Bridge

Page 135

1. Jimmy "The Gerbil" Johnson
2. Fran "Freckleface" Franklin
3. Jean "The Bean" McClean
4. Falona "Baloney" Maloney
5. Shrimpy "The Shrimp" Shrimpton

Page 136